INSPIRE

Grace

Inspiring Stories of God's Gracious Character

12/2019

Mary & Bernie,
Hope you enjoy! My story
is on pg. 7.
Love,
Barbara Todd

INSPIRE
Grace
Inspiring Stories of God's Gracious Character

Edited by Michelle Janene & Dana Sudboro

INSPIRE PRESS
Sacramento, CA

HOPE AND GRACE ON DEATH ROW

Loretta Sinclair

"Chicken. Fried chicken. Cheesecake with strawberries."

"Okay. Drink?"

"Whiskey."

"Sorry," the guard says. "No alcohol with your last meal."

"Whatever." I pace my cell. The six by nine feet that's been home for the last decade will be empty in eighty-nine minutes. Death Row. My room will be open at midnight. Another inmate will move in, and the routine will begin again. There's always a waiting line.

"How 'bout pie?" an inmate yells.

"No pie!" I yell back. I want to add, "and mind your own business too," but this *is* their business. Here on the Row, we are each other's business. What one goes through, we all will. And right now, it's my turn. Billy Valentine, grand theft—that went horribly wrong.

"Pastor's ready." The guard still holds the menu. "Anything else? You can have whatever you want."

"What I want is to go back in time and change what I did. Can you do that for me?"

He shakes his head. "Sorry."

I stare at the wall. "Steak, medium rare, and French fries."

"Ketchup?"

"Heck yeah. You ain't civilized if you don't smother 'em in ketchup." We chuckle.

"Okay. I'll get the cook going on this."

The clock ticking grates against my nerves. That's probably why it's there. Some sadistic dirt bag wants to cause mental torture as the last seconds of life tick by. There's always more noise on these nights. Phones ring more. More guards. Supply carts pushed. Doors slam—and that dang clock.

Breathe deep. Stay calm. Don't fight. I die in seventy-four minutes.

God, let me live one more day. Maybe I can turn things around. Hope. I try to keep hope. It keeps fear at bay.

"Dinner is served," the guard says dryly. I feel as cold inside as the slab of cheesecake on the tray. My shaking hands take the tray and I sit on my cot. I don't even get a table. "How about that pastor?" he asks.

"Not now," I say. "I want to eat first." Truth is I am not hungry. Nor am I ready to admit that this is the end. I still hope for a good outcome—to the bitter end.

The phone rings again. Hope lurches up my throat. Could this be it? My stay of execution. I look at the guards with the same question I have asked all week. Is that the governor? Do I get to live? They avoid my gaze. That means no.

Don't panic. There's still time. "Guard," I yell. He comes. "Is my family here?"

"Not time yet."

I jerk the bars. "I want to see my family—*now*." It does no good. But something inside of me is desperately trying to keep control. "Please," I whisper. Sixty-nine minutes.

"You get fifteen minutes with two of them half an hour before you---"

A jolt of panic surges through me.

"Just hold tight. It's almost time." His voice is softened, almost kind. Not my normal guard.

Pacing passes the time. Counting steps calms me down; helps me to sleep on other nights like this, when it was another's turn. Another death, and then another day. Tomorrow the world will forget that I even existed. Fifty-eight minutes.

What is the point? Why do I exist? Can anyone succeed in this messed up world? All I was trying to do was survive. How can taking from people who wouldn't miss it be so wrong?

But then he died. *Not* my fault. I get that if I hadn't robbed him, it would never have happened. But he turned on me. I reacted. He should have just let me take the money. It wouldn't have mattered one bit to him. But no, he charged me and made me do it. It was his fault. Oh, God.

"Pastor's here."

"Hello." He wears a black shirt with a clerical collar, blue jeans and tennis shoes. His hair is long, and he is old. "I came to see if you wanted to talk."

"About what?" I am not in the mood. Forty-six minutes.

"Hope…"

He has me.

"…for the future."

Future? I think you're in the wrong cell, dude. Instead I say, "Go ahead."

I listen, and he tells me about this guy who has been dead for over two thousand years, but is still alive. He died for all the wrong stuff that I did before I did it, so that I could be free. Me, free. No more cages, guards, or other inmates. For all eternity. There is hope. There is a future.

"Okay." Sounds too good to be true. "What's this going to cost?"

There is no cost, he says. The price has been paid, by this living dead man. He gave His life for me. For Me! Makes no sense, but yet, it feels right. It feels like truth.

"What do I do?" I ask.

"Just ask Him to be your friend. Ask Him to forgive you and let you into Heaven with Him. "

"That's it?"

"That's it," he says. "Want me to help you? We can pray together."

"Sure," I say, but the guard interrupts.

"Time's up. Your family's ready."

I'm torn. I want to see my family, but I want to finish this too. Thirty minutes.

"I'll be in the chamber," he says. "Till the end."

I nod and step out of my cage.

Only two can visit. My parents. There's despair in my mother's eyes, and anger in my father's. But they're here, and I'm grateful. Mom cries. Dad barely speaks. He can't get past *why*. I tell Mom about this guy named Jesus. She cries harder.

Time's up. I leave the room with the guards. Fifteen minutes. Time for the death chamber.

A medical cart walks in front of me. The instruments of my death. The guys on Death Row shake my hand as I walk by. They speak but I can't hear. It's like I am in a wind tunnel. Blood is pumping so hard the sound is echoing in my ears. I see the pastor. He smiles and says something. I can't hear. I'm led into a room with glass windows. I see my family. Mom's still crying. So is the family of the victim. "I'm sorry," I say through the glass. They look away. I don't get their forgiveness.

Strong hands push me down onto a gurney. I see a doctor, and other medical people.

Straps tie me down so I cannot move. My arms are forced out to both sides and tied down. I panic. I can't breathe. Tears fall from my eyes. "I'm sorry." I plead with the guards. "Tell them I'm sorry."

"Ask Him to forgive you," the pastor says. "Just ask." The black hood slips over my head, and my world goes dark.

My bones crush with the first blow. I scream. No one cares. Shock and panic set in with the torture. I hear a scream, but it's not me. Another man. My hood is ripped from my head and my vision restored. Another nail is driven through my second hand and into the cross below. I am freezing and nearly naked. The pain is unbearable. My flesh is ripping and bones are breaking. Then my feet are crossed, and a nail is slammed through them. The bones in my feet shatter. I cannot see, I cannot breathe. The pain is excruciating. I try to writhe, but the searing pain is worse.

"This is how murderers die," the soldier spits out.

The skies tear open and lightning rips through it. Thunder booms, shaking the ground beneath us. And torrential rains pour down from the heavens.

I look around. There are two others with me, although one is making no sound. The guards mock him worse them me.

Our heavy crosses are raised and slammed down into holes in the ground. I scream again. We are on display, left to die alone. I have never hurt this bad in my life, but I deserve it. I am a sinner.

"Forgive them, Father, for they know not what they do," The quiet man says. How can He know that? They are killing us, and He prays for forgiveness—for them! Who is this man?

A soldier climbs up a ladder and nails a sign over his head. It says KING OF THE JEWS. People on the ground mock him. "If you are the Messiah, then save yourself." That's when I hear it. Someone said, "Jesus."

"Just ask Him to forgive you," the pastor had said. "It's that simple. Just ask."

"Jesus," I say, "remember me when you come into your kingdom."

He answers. "Truly I tell you, today you will be with me in paradise."

My burden lifts. My heart is light, and it sings within me. The pain is still there, but I can bear it now. His grace has covered me, and I am at peace.

This man will be my King, for all eternity.

Lori is an author, business woman, mother, and lover of God. She makes her home in Northern California with two children, three dogs, and Princess the Cat.

"Teacher, Can We Have Grace Today?"

Barbara Todd

"Teacher, can we have grace today?" a student asked right before lunch one day. Intrigued, as a new volunteer at our local Christian Academy, I wondered what this meant.

So far, I learned that every Friday, the students prepared their goal cards for the following week. The goal cards listed their subjects across the top of the card, and the day of the week down the left side. The student's responsibility included writing in their daily page assignments for each subject, based on where they left off the previous day. I noticed the word "grace" written over some of their page assignments on several different occasions, and wondered what it meant.

I know, as a Christian, grace is God's unmerited favor, but in the context of schoolwork, it puzzled me. When time permitted, I asked the teacher what "grace" meant in this context.

She explained, "This is my way of teaching God's grace to the children in a manner they can understand. I do it for several reasons: it helps reduce stress for some of the children, gives some a break, whether they deserved it or not, or for no reason at all, just like God gives us grace for all those same reasons and more."

I marveled at the great life lesson she imparted to the children daily.

Several months passed before I had the opportunity to see this gift of "grace" applied firsthand. Early one morning, the teacher texted to let me know she had a family emergency and asked me to help the substitute. When I arrived at the school, the principal told me the substitute also had a sudden emergency, so she would help me until another substitute arrived.

All the children needed help that day, which kept us very busy. One boy, in particular, struggled all morning, trying to stay focused. Every few minutes, he had a question, or, he wanted to sharpen his pencil, or he needed to go to the bathroom. A few minutes later, I saw him daydreaming and doodling at his desk, doing everything but his work. At one point, I watched him saunter over to check his answers, and on the way, he talked to, or bothered, the other students along the way. By mid-day, he had completed one subject, when the norm is two to three. I urged him to get busy so he didn't have homework over the weekend. Instead, he continued dawdling.

Towards the end of the day, several children told me the teacher said they get "grace" this weekend, meaning no homework over the weekend.

While waiting for the principal to return to the classroom to discuss this issue, the student who struggled to obey all day, called me to his desk. I glanced at his goal card as I arrived, and rolled my eyes, only three subjects completed when the goal is five by the end of the day. As I contemplated what to do next, he looked up at me and asked, "Teacher, can I have grace today?"

The first thought that popped into my mind was *If anyone in the class did not deserve grace today, it was him. He bothered the other children all day, didn't finish his assignments, and whined all day.*

Just as quickly, another thought jumped in: *Who of us, as God's children, deserves grace?*

None of us deserves grace but God showers us with His grace daily, whether we recognize it or not. He continually blesses us with His unconditional love and grace during our ugly days, as well as our good days.

My thoughts continued: *Who am I to withhold grace from the student who struggled all day?* Maybe he needed it most of all.

"Yes, you can have grace today," I told him with a drag in my voice. He was so happy; he jumped up to hug me.

Later, as I thought about his reaction, God reminded me that we never know what is happening in other people's lives beyond what we see when we are with them. We often make assumptions. I can put on a "good face" when I am hurting, and when someone asks me how I am doing, I say, "Great," instead of asking the person to pray for me.

This incident caused me to ask myself, *Who do I withhold grace from because the person didn't act the way I thought they should? Did I try to talk to them or encourage them? Or, did I just notice the negative about them?*

I asked the Lord to help me be more aware of those in need of grace, as much as He is attentive to my need for grace daily.

Is there anyone in your life that needs grace today?

Barbara Todd lives in Red Rock, Texas with her husband and farm animals. She loves writing devotionals and Life Lesson stories that the Lord shows her through everyday experiences. Several devotionals are published on line and she is working on a Legacy Book of the stories for her grandchildren.

A Work of Art

Heather D. Blackman

Life's story is like a tapestry.
A masterful creator envisions splendid colors
With distinctive designs.
A stunning work of art.
Yet, amid the magnificent pattern,
The big picture is often obscured
By interlacing feelings of distress,
Depletion, deficiency, and defeat.
But when viewed from God's eyes,
The image becomes clear
As His unmerited favor can be seen
Tightly woven through each intricate detail of life.
Covering, comforting, and carrying you.
And each difficult moment,
Entwined with God's grace,
Is cohesively threaded together

To shape and stretch you,

Into who you were designed to be.

A one-of-a-kind original.

Fashioned by His love,

Purposed for His will.

A beautifully and wonderfully made,

Work of Art!

Heather D. Blackman is honored to share her creative spirit through her passion for writing poetry. Her poems have been published in **Inspire Promise, Inspire Forgiveness, Inspire Joy, Inspire Love,** *and* **Inspire Kindness***. Heather desires that her poetry will uplift, encourage, and express the love of our Heavenly Father.*

BLINDED TO HIS GRACE

James Burgess

As I read my morning devotions, I contemplated what the Apostle Paul meant when he wrote: *For this thing I besought the Lord thrice, that it might depart from me. And he said unto me, My grace is sufficient for thee: for my strength is made perfect in weakness. Most gladly therefore will I rather glory in my infirmities, that the power of Christ may rest upon me.* (2 Corinthians 12:8-9 KJV)

I thought of what Paul wanted removed. I assumed it was a weakness in his eyesight from when he was blinded on the road to Damascus, or it could have been another flaw he saw in his life. This weakness might have been my story. If so, I would not be a writer today. How would God's grace throughout my life be impacted if He had chosen that path for me? Paul's life and mine are similar, but only to a point. However, this simple passage hit me like a two-by-four to the noggin.

When I was in the eighth grade, I had an astigmatism and needed to wear glasses for reading. I felt humiliated. We had just been released for recess from my English class. I hated English, and I did not want to read *Romeo and Juliet* by Shakespeare. In fact, I played baseball and ran track. I did not read!

Off came my glasses, and I ran outside to the basketball courts. I was just attempting my jump shot when my world crashed before me. Everything went immediately black and pain shot through both eyes. I panicked. Terror flooded me.

Another student had thrown a stick and it struck me in my right eye. The dirt from the stick went into my left eye. I couldn't see. The school nurse tried to clean my eyes as best as she could, but to no avail. They rushed me to the emergency room.

The doctor wasn't holding out much hope when he told my parents of the damage.

Total darkness is frightening, especially for an eighth-grader. Reading *Romeo and Juliet* was not a priority, not now or, possibly, in the future.

On the first day, the total dark and bleak picture before me did not look promising. They gently cleansed the grit under the eyelids—gooped ointments and salves—plastered the lids shut—wrapped my eyes with gauze.

I could hear the fear in my parent's voices as they sat beside me the entire night. My parents were not strong Christians. Nevertheless, I heard their prayers.

If it was scary the first day, the second day was worse. My screams could be heard throughout the hospital. By the end of the day, I wanted to read the sports page of the local paper. I take that back. I wanted to read anything.

Finally, on the morning of the third day, I saw gray and got excited. By evening, I could see blurry movement. The fourth morning, a new day dawned. My vision was crystal clear. I headed home with better sight than before the accident and no longer needed glasses.

I had been blind, but now I was healed. Still, I didn't acknowledge God's grace.

Fast forward three years. I still played baseball but focused more on my running skills. I had become a long-distance runner. My sophomore year, I ranked high in the two-mile races. The track coach moved me to the varsity level before the finals. I did very well.

My junior year, I improved. I broke records and it looked as though I might get to the state meet. My problem of rebellion showed its ugly face by the third track meet when a coach caught me and some friends smoking marijuana. They kicked me off the track team and removed my track records. My life spiraled down further into a life of drugs. Over the next two years, I once again became blinded by substance abuse.

God and His grace stepped back into my life through a lovely, Christian young lady who taught me about His abundant grace. You wonder how? She explained she cared a lot about me but wouldn't tolerate my drug life. God was once more gracious to me and freed me from sure death. That young lady has been married to me for forty-six years.

After two years of marriage, I became a Christian. I went all out for God and went to Bible college to become a pastor. Did I have any more lessons to be learned? Yeah, as a pastor, I had a job to do, and like before, I became blind. I had become task-oriented and had no compassion for others' sins. Shouldn't a pastor care for the flock? Well, yes, he should.

I didn't have time to coddle them. My response to my flock, "Here's the Bible—here's your sin—here's the solution—fix it. God's grace is enough for you. Now leave, I have work to do."

Even my prayer life had become part of the job. My time with the Lord had moved to saying, "Lord, bless this work that I have accomplished." I had work to do and all I needed was for Him to make it prosperous. Why did I need His direction? Didn't He send me to Bible college to be trained by others who had the experience? I had this covered.

Five years into the pastorate, the bottom dropped out from under me. I had a self-imposed work pressure breakdown and left the ministry in humiliation.

I ran away in my personal shame, blind to His grace. Where did I run? I ran straight into another of His teaching moments. Like David after his success with Goliath, I got sent back to the sheepfold for more training.

The same day I resigned my position, Jesus showed His grace and provided me with a job. Based on my work record and my previous faith, my former boss, also a Christian, rehired me. However, I continued to hide from the Lord for thirteen years, or so I thought. I hid within my religious outward skin.

My workmates assumed I was an example of Christ, but inwardly, I had been made void and useless for Him. One day, I had an epiphany when a new Christian came to me and thanked me for being an example for him to follow at work. My conscience told me this young man had it all wrong. I knew that my false religious behavior could lead him into a negative life. God had once again pried my blind eyes open to reality, and I could see again. The Lord hid my inner self from others through His grace. I broke down again. This time within my spirit, and I recommitted my life to the Lord.

The rocky road back built new relationships in my marriage, at work, and with Him in particular. He continued to cleanse my eyes with His healing salve. He schooled me through my employment until I was an attentive student.

I prayed that He would once again use me. His grace was enough for me. I had been a blind, broken tool.

Out of nowhere, a fiction story began to form, and I found myself writing it. I had no experience and horrible in most of my English classes. I felt I had no business doing this.

I found His plan had me doing something that highlighted my inadequacies. I became totally dependent upon Him. He shortened my wait until retirement, opening doors to a whole new world of adventure. He introduced me to others I would need to depend on to show me the way. I reached a point where I couldn't just do my job to be successful. I had to lean wholly on Him.

This morning through my devotions, I re-evaluated this blindness and found His grace for me was to retrain me into the servant He originally wanted me to be.

I saw major points in my life where I had been blind more so than when an eighth grader. I spent two years watching as my wife taught me His grace through her daily walk with Him before He mercifully gave me His salvation. Two years learning of His grace before He opened my eyes to His call to ministry. For five years, He gave me the teaching of godly men in Bible college. Five more years He allowed me to minister before He opened my blind eyes to my rebellion. Despite my wicked heart, He gave me a good name and a decent job where I could heal, and my eyes would open again. For twenty-six more years He graciously taught me to be dependent on Him before He returned me to His service through writing.

He gave me forty years of training to see through my blindness, and I'm still learning. I continue to pray for my spiritual blindness to be completely healed, but I will be pleased to live with His grace all sufficient.

James is a graduate of Baptist Bible College, Springfield, MO. Retired knife-grinder from a molding plant after thirty-three years. Contributor to the **Inspire Love** *and* **Inspire Kindness** *anthologies. He is currently preparing to present a book proposal for his second finished novel. He has been married forty-six years to his best friend.*

HEAVEN'S VIEW OF GRACE

Michelle Janene

Tell them the LORD looked down
from his heavenly sanctuary.

He looked down to earth from heaven
to hear the groans of the prisoners,
to release those condemned to die.

(Psalm 102:19-20 NLT)

Zadkiel ambled along the gleaming path noting the reflection of the trees. His gaze rose to the large empty structure not far away. Father never did anything without a purpose, but the many rooms housed within held nothing. Maybe when Master returned, he'd ask about them.

A commotion drew Zadkiel's attention. The Host was raising an uproar. More of his fellow angels were racing to see what was going on. He joined them and peered down to the earth. Master was in trouble again. His hands were bound. The words the humans shouted made Zadkiel's heart cringe.

Zadkiel and the others leaned over the edge of heaven further as the men began to beat their Master.

"Surely Father will send us soon to tend to Him, as we did before," Zadkiel said. No one seemed to be listening. Master had suffered many days and had to face that snake Lucifer. But when the fallen wretch had been sent packing, Zadkiel and others of the ministering angels had traveled to earth and cared for Master. They'd fed him and restored him. Father was sure to send them again. Any moment now.

Zadkiel turned and looked for Father. He stood a little way off, watching but not closely. Father seemed...resolute, determined. But He didn't send any of them down to protect His Son.

Shouts from the Host turned Zadkiel's attention back to the events. They rattled their weapons ready to charge to Master's defense. But they weren't sent either.

The humans nailed Master to a cross.

What was happening? Why was Father allowing this? Master hung there. Blood dripped from His many wounds. He struggled to draw in a breath. The gasps for air grew shallower as the time between each lengthened.

"My God, My God, why have You forsaken Me?" Master cried.

Zadkiel turned. Father was walking away, his back turned to the anguish of His Son.

Heaven fell silent. The angels looked at one another as Master breathed His last breath with His earthly form.

Father, Master, and Comforter had never been apart. Then Master went to earth, became a human born of a created woman. Now Father and Master had been separated.

The praise of the cherubim in the temple silenced. Father had not returned there. No beings in all of heaven made a sound.

A clash of weapons rose in the stillness.

The great rending of metal tore through the air. The gates of that traitor Lucifer were wrenched open, freeing those he had tried to steal from Father.

Here in heaven, time had no meaning, but days seemed to pass on the world below. Those who followed Master on earth wept. Zadkiel wanted to as well.

A long line of saints rose from the depths robed in fine white linen. Master followed later clothed in brilliant glory.

Father stood at the gates. The giant pearl entrances had never been opened. Master carried the key—red like the blood He had shed.

Father, Son, and Comforter embraced as the Host began a triumphant victory shout that shook all of heaven. Then, one by one, Master introduced those He'd brought with Him to the Father they had believed but never seen. Father greeted each with a new name and welcomed them with such love.

Adam, Eve, Noah, Abraham, Joseph, Daniel, and all the ones who had trusted Father came into heaven and began to fill the many-roomed structure.

"What's going on?" Zadkiel asked of those gathered around him looking on.

"Grace has come to man," Father said as He walked with His children. They laughed and worshiped so much, they drowned out the praise of the cherubim.

"Zadkiel," Master waved him over. "Prepare all the ministering angels. Soon you will be called upon to tend those who will be persecuted for My name's sake. And there will be many."

"Master, what is grace?" Zadkiel asked.

"It was what We had planned from the beginning of time to save our people from their sins. Our people no longer stand condemned. I paid their debt and now they are free." Master followed in the wake of all the newcomers as those gathered around Zadkiel burst into rapid chatter.

"Grace! The plan to set humans free."

"Master took their sins."

"The gates of heaven are open. The captives have been made free."

Zadkiel moved from the others, pondering Master's great work. It was not what he had expected, but as always, it was the perfect solution. He gazed back to the earth as word spread among the humans that Master had risen and been seen by many. Comforter left and placed His presence in every soul that believed in the grace that had been given.

Many were joyous at the gift Master had given and many were angry at those who trusted in the one the humans called the Christ. Already many were in danger.

Master was right. Zadkiel was sent to comfort those who the world hated all because of grace.

I was chosen to explain to everyone this mysterious plan that God, the Creator of all things, had kept secret from the beginning. God's purpose in all this was to use the church to display his wisdom in its rich variety to all the unseen rulers and authorities in the heavenly places. This was his eternal plan, which he carried out through Christ Jesus our Lord. (Ephesians 3:9-11 NLT)

Michelle Janene has authored seven fiction books, been included in the Inspire anthologies, writes a monthly advice column for **Pandora's Box Gazette,** *and oversees two critique groups. As a writer she hopes to reach those who feel they are unseen. Learn more at* www.michellejanene.com

Hannah:
Surrendering When God Is Silent

Debbie Jones Warren

> *The Lord makes poor and makes rich;*
> *he brings low and he exalts.*
> *He raises up the poor from the dust;*
> *he lifts the needy from the ash heap.*
> (1 Samuel 2:7-8 ESV)

For thirty years my parents served as missionaries in Nigeria where they raised five children. When I turned six, I started attending boarding school, only returning home for summer and Christmas vacations. I frequently felt homesick, lonely, and scared. While the other kids played, joked, and laughed boisterously, many times I was so upset I couldn't even eat. I begged my parents to teach me at home, but that wasn't an option.

Every year, I asked God to rescue me from boarding school, and my mom prayed for a better solution for my education. Yet, year after year, I climbed into the single-engine Piper Comanche that flew me back to dorm life. I felt like God didn't hear me.

Has there been a time in your life when you felt desperate? When you prayed day and night for the situation, but God didn't seem to hear, because the trial continued for a long, long time? You may still be in the middle of the battle.

When God is Silent

The story of Hannah in the Old Testament showcases a woman with an unanswered prayer. Hannah was dearly loved by her husband, Elkanah, but she had one great, unfilled longing: she wanted a child. Elkanah took a second wife, Peninnah, who bore him many children, but she treated Hannah as an adversary and ridiculed, mocked, and tormented her.

Elkanah comforted Hannah, saying, "Why are you downhearted? Don't I mean more to you than ten sons?" He declared that Hannah meant everything to him, with or without children. Additionally, Elkanah was pointing out that although she had good reason to be troubled, did it justify being troubled to this extent? Sorrow isn't sinful, unless it crowds out contentment or leads us to doubt God's grace.

Except for fifth grade and twelfth grade, I lived in a dorm during all my school years. I gradually became accustomed to life at boarding school and learned to get along by obeying the rules. But I grew to resent my parents for not being around when I needed them. In junior high, I began to pull away from them emotionally.

In June 1976, my family moved back to the U.S. for my senior year in high school. When I began college, my mom and dad returned to their work in Nigeria and left me to navigate into adulthood on my own. For decades I struggled with confusion and loneliness resulting from long separations from family and lack of their personal, timely input.

Over time, I rebelled against their faith and plunged into the partying lifestyle, experimenting with everything that went with it. I quit attending church and reading my Bible because I didn't find many relatable examples of God's love, joy, or grace.

Sometimes God appeared downright mean. For example, the account of Hannah giving her young son to God and sending him to live in the tabernacle, seemed like an example justifying my parents' decision to send me off to boarding school for most of my formative years.

During those difficult years, I felt like God was indifferent to my pain. He didn't strike me as the gracious, loving Father my childhood Sunday school teachers had declared he was.

Hannah's Surrender

Hannah, despite all her troubles, didn't complain, nag, turn bitter, or turn away from God, but allowed her pain to drive her into His heart. She acknowledged God's sovereignty, even while she expressed her pain. Yes, she prayed for her circumstances to change, but clung to faith in God's wisdom and goodness.

However, this woman who was the epitome of grace-under-pressure finally came to her breaking point. She had persevered a long, long time through the hardship, but eventually, the torment by the other wife upset her so much she couldn't eat.

At the tabernacle, Hannah poured out her heart to God, vowing if He would grant her a son, she would give him to the Lord. Eli the priest blessed her saying, "Go in peace, and may the God of Israel grant you what you have asked of him." He didn't promise a child, but Hannah felt heard by God, and that calmed her heart.

The next morning the family worshiped together before returning home. There Hannah gave thanks to God, even before she received her miracle.

Do I believe that God's grace is enough, even without seeing His gifts or His healing? In the problems I struggle with today, even if God is silent, I know He hasn't forgotten me. My loving heavenly Father sees me, cares for me, and walks my path with me. Like Hannah, I can let my pain drive me into God's loving arms and trust that He will answer and give what is best for me.

God's Provision

After I graduated from Fresno State in 1983, my boyfriend, Chris, proposed. I wrote my parents, shared my happy news, and asked if they could take an early furlough and help me prepare for our wedding. Mom and Dad happily did so.

Even better, they decided to remain in the States, instead of returning to overseas ministry. Through God's gracious provision, the mission board created a new ministry position at UC Berkeley for my parents to serve among the many international students there. I lived in a town just twenty minutes away.

As my three children, Andrew, Heather, and Robby, came along, my parents cleared their schedule each time I needed childcare. My prayers for connection with my parents were answered at long last.

Over a period of eighteen years, I experienced my mom and dad lavishing all the love on my kids that I missed out on. Even though God didn't rescue me from that boarding school, He had not forgotten me.

We'll always have problems: Life won't ever be perfect. Hannah had to give up her son, yet she poured out a remarkable song of praise to God as she left Samuel behind. Even though the separation was undoubtedly difficult, she didn't regret the vow she'd made.

In her song, she acknowledged God's holiness, goodness, and wisdom, and applauded the way He governed the world. The insights Hannah expressed show us how thoroughly she had searched the Scriptures and cried out to God for understanding of her situation. She found it. Through suffering, we often experience a deepened connection with our Savior, resulting from countless hours spent calling out to the Lord and combing through the Bible for His promises.

I believe God chose to allow the separation, neglect, and grief in my childhood for His good reasons. He didn't close his eyes or lose attention while my lonely years slipped by unnoticed. He is sovereign over everything that happens to me and loves me fiercely. His grace is sufficient for supplying everything I need.

During times of suffering, He sees me, loves me, and constantly cares for me. I've learned from Hannah's life that God is always sovereign, even when He seems silent.

And the meaning of Hannah's name? *Grace.*[1]

Born in Alameda, California, Debbie Jones Warren moved to Nigeria with her missionary parents before her first birthday. Now in Castro Valley, she and husband, Chris, love time with their amazing adult children and their oldest son's girlfriend. Debbie enjoys cooking gluten-free, learning German, and hosting garden teas for friends.

---

[1] This article was previously published June 2, 2008 on Debbie's blog debbiejoneswarren.com

THE LANGUAGE OF GRACE

Judith Ingram

It was the final evening of my first writer's conference. We stood in a nervous circle, six unpublished authors taking turns describing our pet writing projects, floating our cherished ideas on an untried audience and hoping for approval. When my turn came, I glanced around the circle of expectant faces and felt my cheeks warm.

"I've been working on a book about forgiveness," I said. "It explores what forgiveness means, why we need it, and how we can begin to practice it." I saw interest spark around the group and some heads nodding. Encouraged, I went on to explain some of my ideas and my hopes for reaching an audience through speaking as well as writing. All seemed to agree that forgiveness was an important topic.

I was enjoying the cross-conversation when my attention caught on a woman who had joined our group. "Olivia*," according to her name badge, was a large woman who stood with feet planted firmly apart and arms folded tightly across her chest. She cleared her throat.

"I don't do forgiveness," she said. "I don't believe in it." Her words sliced into the circle and silenced the group. The others looked at her, at each other, and then every face turned toward me. Olivia's dark eyes fixed me with a smoldering challenge.

Scripture tells us that only God knows a person's heart. Nevertheless, I recognized the pain that fueled her anger, saw it in her defensive stance, heard it in her defiant words. Sympathy sprang up in me, and in that moment my pet writing project became something bigger.

I fell back on my practiced elevator speech, but she interrupted me. "That's fine for you," she said. "But were you *molested?*"

There it was, the root of her pain, and mine, too. My cheeks burned again as I struggled to decide whether I could acknowledge in front of these strangers the shame and torment that had kept me in therapy for nine years. Then in a flash, I knew with certainty that God had a gift for this woman, and He wanted me to deliver it.

I looked her full in the face and said quietly, "Yes. By my father."

She considered me for a long moment. The group collectively held its breath. I can't say what happened in her heart, but I saw her body relax, her expression soften. She nodded. "Then you and I can talk," she said.

As if on cue, the others drifted away, leaving us alone. For the next half-hour or so, Olivia and I stood together in a corner of that crowded, noisy room, sharing our stories. She confessed how she longed for peace but clung to anger and resentment to keep her safe from further harm. Although she was not a believer, she listened to my story of God's work in my life and how forgiving my family became an essential part of living a deeper faith and learning to love despite human cruelties. We cried together and embraced before she left me and retired to her hotel room.

As I recall this experience, I realize that God gifted me to speak to this woman in much the same way as He did the believers who were gathered together at Pentecost waiting for the Holy Spirit Jesus had promised them. With a tremendous noise and wind from heaven that brought people running, the Spirit filled that group of believers and gifted them with languages to speak to every foreigner in Jerusalem. Jews from every nation gathered and in amazement exclaimed, *"We all hear these people speaking in our own languages about the wonderful things God has done!"* (Acts 2:11 NLT). That day God poured out grace through the believers to bless and give witness to the good news of God's mercy and love.

Through my experience of abuse and recovery, God showed me a path of grace and forgiveness and gave me language to speak to others who have been similarly hurt. This dear woman had asked me, in effect, "Do you speak my language of hurt and betrayal?" She wanted to know if I could understand and relate to her native experience of family molestation. Only then could she trust my words and consider my message of comfort and hope in Jesus.

Each of us longs to converse in our native tongue, that is, in the language of our personal experience. Support groups such as Alcoholics Anonymous are effective because individuals, desperate for change, look for hope among others who bear similar scars and share similar stories of desperation and regret. People listen for words that have meaning for them, for narratives that offer practical help and inspiration for a better way of life.

When we speak the language of God's grace in our lives, listeners may be moved by the Spirit to ask, like the crowds at Pentecost, *"What should we do?"* (Acts 2:37 NLT). I sensed this very question hovering between Olivia and me as we spoke together, but it never quite surfaced.

The next morning, I sat at a table with others eating breakfast when someone touched me on the shoulder. I looked up and met Olivia's intense gaze. "I'm still thinking about what you said," she offered. She gave my shoulder a quick squeeze and hurried away before I could respond. The conference broke up at noon, and I never saw her again.

Language is a gift from God, one of the attributes we humans share with Him. Our words are like seeds God uses to dispense grace wherever grace is needed. I will never know what happened to those seeds of grace I shared with Olivia that evening. I do know that only God can take ugly, hurtful memories and transform them into something beautiful—a narrative God uses to speak into the hearts of others who have suffered a similar pain and who need to hear the offer of God's redemptive healing in a language they can understand.

*not her real name

*Judith Ingram is the author of **A Devotional Walk with Forgiveness** and posts weekly devotionals on her blog. A survivor of childhood abuse herself, she loves to speak and write about how to practice God's love in relationships. Judith lives with her husband in the San Francisco East Bay.*

SUFFICIENT GRACE

Ellen Cardwell

> *"My grace is sufficient for you,*
> *for my strength is made perfect in weakness."*
> (2 Corinthians 12:9 NKJV)

I lay on my back, dreading the painful exercises the doctor prescribed. I wouldn't completely recover from knee surgery unless I did them. The effort seemed daunting. I stared at the ceiling, procrastinating.

Finally, I asked God for help. A Scripture came to mind, *My grace is sufficient for you, for My strength is made perfect in weakness.* I didn't think about the context, or the difference in Paul's situation, or how other Christians often suffer worse conditions than mine. Instead, I took the words to mean God's strength would help my weakened body do the recommended workout.

I accepted the encouragement, began one set, completed it, and rested. Then began another one and another until I completed them all. Despite the medication, it *hurt*. God didn't remove the pain, but He helped me through it.

Looking back, I recalled how He enabled me to overcome other weaknesses. Usually, Scripture was involved. God provided the verse, I followed it as though He instructed me, and together we dealt with the problem. His strength was the grace I needed at the time. Not once did He fail to show up, and on the basis of that history, I'm able to expect His help whenever I need it most.

I love how our gracious High Priest helps us without making us feel "less than." He experienced human nature, understands our weaknesses, and invites us to bring our inadequacies to Him. When we do, our Lord *will* step into our circumstances, and we will come through stronger by His sufficient grace.

Ellen's fondness for books began with children's classics and developed through many visits to the library, where she later worked during her school years. Eventually, she penned notes, wrote newsletters, and created ad copy, all of which segued into writing professionally. Inspirational and non-fiction articles are among her published works.

A Word from Hope

Julie Blackman

Carla was excited to finally have a Wednesday off so she could attend the six o'clock Bible study. Carla arrived early, walked to the middle row of seats in the room, and sat down. She didn't like being on display at the front, and neither did she appreciate the constant chatter from the women in the back rows. Carla shuffled in her seat to get comfortable as her cell phone buzzed. She grabbed her handbag and frantically searched for the phone. It was a text message from her coworker, Ashley, asking if Carla could cover her 7:00 p.m. to 7:00 a.m. shift that night. Ashley must have assumed Carla would oblige and had already notified their nurse manager. It was a little presumptuous, but Carla did mention the day before that she needed some extra hours. Carla affirmed she could cover Ashley.

Typical, now I'll have to leave the Bible study early. Luckily, the church, her home, and the hospital were all near each other. She could stay for the first twenty minutes and still have time to go home, throw on some scrubs, and get to the hospital by 7:00 p.m.

Carla bowed her head as Maureen, the Bible study leader, opened the meeting with prayer.

"Amen. Before we get started," Maureen said, "I feel led by the Lord to ask if anyone would like to share with the group right now?" Maureen paused and glanced around the room.

A woman about two rows in front of Carla raised her hand. Carla didn't recognize her.

"Would you mind coming up to the front?" Maureen asked with a smile. "I don't think we've seen you here before. Is this your first time?"

"Yes. I recently moved to Colorado," the woman said, making her way to the front of the room.

"Welcome, welcome. And thank you for sharing. Your name is?"

"Hi everyone, my name is Hope. My mother says she gave me this name because she didn't think she could have children. Then out of the blue, I showed up."

Everyone laughed. It was a great ice breaker.

"Okay, Hope, take it away." Maureen patted Hope on the shoulder and walked to her seat in the front row.

Carla stared at Hope intently, who was wearing denim capris, a brightly colored flowery top and the cutest strappy sandals she'd seen. Hope appeared to be in her early to mid-forties. Her hair had silvery threads of gray among glossy dark brown curls. She was undoubtedly a Fashionista because everything matched down to her jewelry accessories and her multi-colored framed glasses.

"I was brought up in a Christian home," Hope said. "It was just my mother and me. Many times I heard my mother praying, 'God, please give me the grace to go through this so Hope can see Your faithfulness.' She explained how God's ultimate demonstration of grace was when He sent His Son to die on the cross for our sins. But that His grace doesn't stop there. It comes in many forms such as protection, strength, and courage to sustain you. And when things got tough for us, I witnessed God give my mother grace time and time again. I am blessed to have a mother with a deep faith in God."

Carla nodded her head in agreement, thinking of her mother, who personified the characteristics of a Proverbs 31 woman.

"I know what it means to trust God," Hope continued. "And I know I can count on Him to bring me through the bad times. I'm not sure who this is intended for tonight, but I want to let you know God loves you. He wants the best for you. So, don't waste your time thinking about the coulda, shoulda, wouldas, and focusing on your current circumstances. You'll miss out on the blessings He has for you. In everything, give God thanks. And always remember, the Great I Am is in control. Things may not go the way you planned, but then your plan doesn't really matter—only His does. And trust me, God has a plan for your life."

Hope paused to take a breath and turned to face Carla.

"Ask Him to show you His will and then obey Him. Be steadfast and know that whatever happens, God's grace is sufficient. You're not alone. Well, thank you so much for letting me share." Hope glanced at Maureen, smiled, and returned to her seat.

Tears streamed down Carla's face. She needed to hear this. She'd spent the better part of the day complaining about how her life didn't turn out the way she'd hoped. If only she used this time to count her blessings, then she'd realize and focus on God's goodness. God had helped her numerous times. What did she have to gripe about? She has a home, a vehicle, a decent paying job, and her health. Carla bowed her head whispering praises to God and asking for forgiveness.

"Thank you so much, Hope. That was wonderful," Maureen said and shared what God had done for her this week.

Carla checked the time on her cell phone and discreetly motioned to Maureen that she had to leave.

As she walked out of the room and across the parking lot to her car, she thought about Hope. *Who was she, an angel sent from God?*

Carla got into her car and sat for a few minutes. She realized she was meant to hear what Hope had to say. Thankfully, Maureen was obedient to God by inviting people to share at the beginning of the Bible study. Otherwise, Carla would have missed out.

Carla started the car, and her favorite hymn began to play over the radio: "Amazing Grace." Tears flowed down her face as she sang along. *This is precisely how God works. When you need encouragement, strength, or even a little push to keep going, He will send you help and the grace to get you through.*

"Thank you, dear Lord, for never giving up on me. Help me to be the servant you want me to be."

Carla wiped her eyes. Then she looked in the rear-view mirror for oncoming cars, pulled out of the parking spot, and drove home.

*Julie Blackman writes nonfiction and fiction inspirational pieces. Her work is published in **Inspire Victory, Inspire Promise, Inspire Forgiveness, Inspire Love, Inspire Joy,** and **Inspire Kindness**. Julie also writes for FaithWriters.com. Her passion for writing has grown and writing about the Lord is her desire.*

A God of Justice

Cheríe Denna

The judge assigned to my case peered at me over the frame of his reading glasses. "Miss LaLanne, I could hold you in contempt of court for this. You know that, right?"

"Yes, Your Honor."

"Well, it seems more fitting to suspend your parenting rights for one weekend," he said as he turned his attention to my ex-husband's lawyer.

"Mr. Foster, are you in agreement?" The judge began scrolling our parenting calendar. Our co-parenting arrangement alternated weekends. Our daughter was already with her father for most weekdays. Since I was on restricted probation, it was easier for him to get her to and from school.

I cringed at the thought of losing more time with my daughter. That meant we would not have another weekend together for an entire month. On the other hand, I knew the consequences of my choices could have been much worse, so I remained quiet.

His attorney responded, "Yes, my client agrees this is fitting and requests the court suspend the weekend of May tenth from Angelica's mother."

Checking the calendar, the judge replied, "That happens to be Mother's Day weekend. You are suspending her from having Mother's Day with her daughter?"

I looked over at my ex-husband with intense hatred, yet disbelief. He could not even look at me. I wanted to hurt him. *How could he do this?* I tried to maintain my composure. The tears poured down my face. *What would my angel babe think of me now?*

"It seems fitting, Your Honor," his lawyer scoffed.

The fact that I was fighting to hold onto my parenting rights was surreal. It took five years of In Vitro Fertilization (IVF) before having my one and only child. I'll never forget the day my infertility was diagnosed. When I asked the doctor how my fallopian tubes ended up so disfigured and riddled with scar tissue, he could not give a conclusive answer. He did, however, question me about my sexual history.

"Yes, I was molested as a child." I couldn't believe I was having this conversation.

My doctor went on to describe the probability of silent infections causing the massive destruction to my reproductive system. "The only way you'll conceive is through In Vitro Fertilization."

I was furious. Furious at my stepfather. Furious at God. I needed a moment alone to process all of this. Not only was this yet another trauma to my soul, but rage welled up in me as I worked through the emotional triggers that accompanied this news. I screamed as I cried into my hands. "He stole my childhood and now he gets to steal my motherhood, too?"

Our life took a sudden turn as we navigated our reality as an infertile couple. IVF was still considered experimental. There were no guarantees and zero insurance coverage for the procedure. We financed our home and scrimped and saved to pay for the astronomical costs. The first two IVF cycles were devastating. We were ready to give up.

I needed answers. Was Jesus the answer? A dear friend of mine invited me to attend a Christian women's retreat with her church in the Santa Cruz mountains. There, I was on my knees, crying out to Jesus. *Are you real? Do you even care? Why am I going through this?*

Several ladies prayed for me. "Cherie, are you ready to accept Jesus Christ as your Lord and Savior? All you have to do is ask Him into your heart and pray this prayer."

After we prayed together, I stood in awe of what took place. *Is this for real?* We started singing songs to God. In that moment, I was overcome with peace in my soul. All the rage and fear left me. One of the women seated near me handed me a card with a handwritten Scripture from the Bible, *For I know the plans I have for you, says the Lord, they are plans for good and not for disaster, to give you a future and a hope.* (Jeremiah 29:11 NLT)

My new faith gave me the strength to endure the third and final attempt at IVF. This was my first experience learning how to trust God. During my prayer time, it was as if Jesus was speaking to me. "My child, he will not steal this from you. I am a God of justice." This changed everything. I believed in my heart we would be blessed with a baby.

The following year, God entrusted me with the most miraculous of gifts. I was now a mother. When she was dedicated to the Lord, I vowed to raise her up in His teachings.

As time went on, I began battling PTSD. My marriage fell apart and I lost myself. From there, I returned to what was familiar from my childhood. The outlaw biker clubs were easy to track down. I did anything and everything to be accepted and taken under their protective covering. The sexual addiction and promiscuity I struggled with early on in life returned with a vengeance. I would prove my loyalty to the clubs using any means necessary. That included tattooing my body, having sex, theft, whatever. It was dangerous. I nearly went to prison, but my public defender saw that I did not belong in jail. Mercy. Grace.

My daughter was only eight years old and she hated everything about me and my lifestyle. My choices caused me to lose my house and everything else we had worked so hard to build. And I was now on the verge of losing my daughter. Her father was very vindictive and was determined to get full physical and legal custody. My life had taken a bad turn and I certainly was not faithful to my vow to God concerning my precious daughter. I was awful at promises to anyone.

Our family court case was into its fifth painful year. Our daughter endured so much trauma through mediation, counselors, and fights between her father and me. I determined to straighten my life out and I recommitted my life to the Lord during this time. Despite this, my ex-husband pulled out the heavy artillery in the courtroom. His lawyer began manufacturing lies and embellishing the truth. Things were bad enough, but the picture he began painting of me was filled with lie after lie.

Throughout these years in court, I represented myself. There was no legal representation available if you did not have the money to hire one. I spent hours on end in the law library each week, researching forms and legal procedures. No matter what lie was fabricated against me, I was not giving up my fight for my child. I began researching parental alienation and learned how to best respond to emergency ex parte orders. Those are court orders served without notice. I was doing all this on my own resources.

While praying one night, and reading from my Bible, I came to a Scripture that read, *But don't be afraid of those who threaten you. For a time is coming when everything that is covered will be revealed, and all that is secret will be made known to all."* (Matthew 10:26 NLT). I remembered reading how God is a God of justice and truth. *Oh, Lord, please show me grace and reveal Your truth in the courtroom.* I thanked God for this Word. *I need to pray this Scripture in the courtroom.* I believed if I prayed and declared this Scripture over my court case, over every courtroom, and over everyone involved in the case, truth would prevail.

Once I began praying that Scripture in the courtroom, over the lawyer, the judge, and even the bailiff, strange things began happening in the courthouse. My ex-husband's lawyer, who vowed to never let me see my daughter again, began making a fool of himself in the clerk's office. He was even reprimanded in the courtroom. One morning, I responded to another emergency ex parte hearing. While waiting for my hearing, the clerk told me the lawyer did not file the necessary forms and that I could go home.

The lawyer chased me down the hallway, yelling, "Stop! You better not go out that door!"

Security ended up reporting him to the court.

At our next scheduled hearing, we found out a new judge had been assigned to the case. I was not sure what to think. *He's not even familiar with my case or anything I have presented. What now?*

The judge took a few minutes to quickly look through our case file before addressing us. "I can't believe how long this case has been dragging on. I do not see anything proving this mother is unfit. All custody orders will remain as is. This case is dismissed. Good luck to you both."

What just happened? I sat there in awe of God with tears running down my face.

"Thank you, Your Honor."

I closed my eyes and thanked God for His justice and for His Word.

Cherie Denna is a writer and blogger who is passionate about the power of telling her story. Having been rescued from a family of organized crime and outlaw biker clubs, her life is a testimony to the redemptive power of Jesus Christ. Writing retreats at the ocean are her favorite.

YOUR GRACE

Susan McCrea

Your grace is sufficient unto me.
Your grace is sufficient unto me.
Your strength is made perfect in weakness in me.
Your grace is sufficient unto me.

My grace is sufficient unto thee.
My grace is sufficient unto thee.
My strength is made perfect in weakness in thee.
My grace is sufficient unto thee.
My strength is made perfect in weakness in thee.
My grace is sufficient unto thee.

This is a song/poem, based on 2 Corinthians 12:9 KJV, and received during a recent trial.

Susan McCrea lives with her husband, Martin, in Fair Oaks where they raised seven children and welcome visits from their fifteen-plus grandchildren. The book about her adoption discovery at thirty-eight and reunion with her birth family twenty years later is almost completed. Contact her for information about it at scm777@sbcglobal.net.

GRACE DELIVERS DADDY'S LOVE -
MISTY'S STORY

Tessa Bertoldi

———⟨❦⟩———

I was very bitter and upset as I was planning my wedding. I felt cheated of a real Dad. My father had a long history of abusing me, neglecting me, and forgetting important events like my birthday and all my school graduations. He abused my mother until a long white Ford Bronco drive shown on TV changed the justice system's attitude on domestic violence. My paternal grandfather bullied and punished me as well and never showed love. He was mean and hateful with words, money, and emotions. It was a relief to many when he passed on.

My maternal grandfather was loved by everyone. Even though he died before I was born, I felt like I knew him and was loved by him, the difference was a Grand Canyon in my growing up years. My biological father and biological grandfather chose to bully me and were not interested in my happiness. Instead, God gave me the gift of my step-dad and step-grandpa. (Mother taught me to drop the steps and focus on the love instead, so from here on, I will).

Dad's passing so near to my wedding brought many negative feelings back about the choices of those that should have loved me. Dad was a kind and loving man, but I was in emotional turmoil as a young girl and woman and did not appreciate it as much when he was still alive. Looking back, he did love me and demonstrated his love to me time and again, even when I was not grateful. He had a way of knowing things and gave grace to ninety-nine percent of the people he met.

I was also loved by my paternal grandmother's husband. Grandpa chose to marry my grandmother and raise her children with all the problems that abused children come with. He was a soft-spoken man, but his words were powerful. Grandpa never belittled or hit and would often have insightful talks with me. He knew from his wife the type of physical and emotional abuse my father had dished out to his mother, wife, and daughter. Grandpa was a calming influence in our lives. He never demanded anything from me.

All I wanted was the fairy tale dream of a daddy walking his little girl down the aisle and the dance with Cinderella scene from the popular song. As the event got closer, everyone feared I would turn into a bridezilla. Then, I realized that I had been given a gift. Grandpa was a true grandfather and graciously offered to walk me down the aisle and to share my first dance. It was an offer extended out of love with no strings attached. He loved me and was aware of the strained relationship between his step-son and the rest of the world. That unconditional offer was what I needed to break through my pain into healing.

It was a process to work through those feelings and emotions and remember the love I had from Dad and still have from Grandpa. When the big day came, a friend of Dad's walked me partially down the aisle and my biological father, who showed up late, walked me the rest of the way. My wedding dance was with Grandpa, and I felt just like the magical Cinderella.

God showed me His great grace by putting these loving men in my life. I didn't deserve their kindness or love. They had no responsibility to me and, at times, I was either withdrawn or sullen. I received what I didn't deserve—grace. Dancing with Grandpa reminded me how truly blessed I was and to focus on what I had and not what I didn't. Accepting the grace of God empowered me to dance with my biological father and show the respect he did not deserve.

I have had the opportunity to act on my faith and to give God's grace back to others. I had two employment positions that lasted less than a year that I called my dys-positions. "Dys" because they were so dysfunctional. The clients were dysfunctional and the administration was highly dysfunctional. Employees spoke meanly of others. Stories about individuals were circulated and exaggerated until there was only a spark of truth at its foundation. People's lives and careers were damaged by "well-meaning" gossips. Management did not take any corrective action to stem this rot from within, and at times participated.

My father and grandfather are masters at taking a small truth, a little bit of information, and turning it into a weapon. They are and were information brokers. A small scratch in a parking lot could easily be turned into the death of someone's character by stretching it into a horrible driver that cannot be trusted. The proof was the car accident in the parking lot. It would not matter that the car was parked legally and unoccupied, *it* was in an accident. A truth that could be stretched into a weapon.

My personal history with abusive information brokers and God's grace, and kind men standing in the gap, gave me the eyes to see and the wisdom to know what was happening around me. I choose to speak kindly of others, even when they do not deserve it. Even when they are on the path to weaponizing information with gossip. It has placed a lot of stress on me, but I pray for God's intervention.

One or two of my co-workers noticed that I would change the subject to a more positive one. I hope they were able to use my example for a good change. God has given me his grace by filling my life with His Love, Dad, and Grandpa, my loving replacements. To those of us who have received grace, we should also give grace. It is God's way.

Great people talk about ideas.

Average people talk about things.

Small people talk about other people.

Author: Unknown

Tessa, full-time technical writer and author, balances her time between writing, fiber art, and practicing gratitude in a sustainable lifestyle. She is on staff for the SF Writers Conference and Writing for Change. Her projects include a post-apocalyptic sci-fi novel, curriculum collaboration, poetry, inspirational shorts, how-to guides, and a light romance.

JESUS AT THE BEACH

Christine Hagion

"I feel like my brain is on fire," my patient CiCi said. She sat across from me in the therapy room, with her feet crossed, and looked down at the brightly colored faux-Persian rug, as though embarrassed.

"What is it that makes you feel that way? Can you describe it to me?" I asked.

Cici straightened her pale gray T-shirt and pulled on her navy-blue cardigan to cover the rolls around her midsection. Her mouth had a permanent downward turn to it, forming what appeared to be an upside-down smile. I reviewed our previous sessions in my mind and pondered, *have I ever seen her smile?*

As CiCi went on talking about her increasing frustration with her co-workers, I took notes. I mentioned that this was a frequent theme we'd discussed over the past year. The names of the colleagues changed from week to week, but only the details differed. She recounted how this one had left fifteen minutes early, and how that one had not completed a list of tasks supposed to have been done during the shift.

"I caught another co-worker playing cards when he was supposed to be stocking the towels." Cici said that he'd looked at her sheepishly when she'd discovered him playing games instead of working. She hadn't mentioned anything to the manager because she didn't want to be a snitch.

Cici tucked a swath of black hair behind her ear. The rest of it hung limply around her face, with a few gray strands framing its squarish shape. I took a sip of my coffee and wondered how many more times we would circle this same mountain.

"I just don't know how I'm supposed to let this stuff go. I feel like I'm ready to explode."

The white noise machine outside the door muffled the sound so other patients could not hear what was being said. It also offered me some privacy in the modes of treatment I employed.

"I have an idea, if you're willing to try a little experiment with me," I offered.

Her head bobbed up and down in agreement.

Although I worked as a therapist in a community mental health setting, I had sometimes invoked Cici's faith in our sessions. Doing so involved some risk on my part, but I trusted that she would not reveal it to the clinic leadership. The Jewish director at the clinic was more open to issues of faith, but my clinical supervisor was opposed to anything that hinted of religion or spirituality.

"I know you're a Christian," I began. "Do you remember what happened in the Gospels when the woman caught in adultery was brought before Jesus?"

Her head wiggled up and down like a bobblehead doll.

"Can you tell me what you remember about it?" This was far more direct and more intense spiritual content than I'd ever ventured before in this setting. When I was counseling at the church, this would have been fine; but this was a secular clinic. *Oh, Lord. I need You to back me up on this!*

"Yeah," she said, and then leaned forward before saying, "They brought her before Him, and they were going to stone her."

The line between her two eyebrows deepened. She looked straight at me, as if bracing for an attack. *I hope she doesn't feel that I am judging her.*

"Yes. Do you recall what He did next?" *I hope this doesn't sound like I'm infantilizing.*

"He bent down and wrote in the sand." Her brow knit, as though she was trying to figure out where I was headed with this.

"Right. And what do you think that was about?" *Gosh, I don't want her to feel like a kid at Sunday School, getting badgered with questions.*

"Some people say He was writing down the sins of her accusers in the sand."

I scanned her briefly to see if this concept was landing with her. Cici looked a little perplexed, but nodded again. *Good. She is still with me.*

"Okay, I want you to close your eyes and picture this: Jesus is bending down, writing in the sand."

She closed her eyes obediently.

I bet she thinks she knows what I will be saying next: something about throwing down stones.

"And now I want you to be kneeling down, right next to Him. And while you are writing in the sand, Jesus is doing the same. Can you picture that?"

She nodded slightly.

"You are writing in the sand the mistakes of your co-workers, and Jesus is writing down your sins." I waited for a moment to let this sink in.

"Now I want you to think of you and Jesus, at the beach. Think of it like a parent, helping their child make a sandcastle. They both are covered in sand, having fun, laughing, and enjoying being with each other.

Making sandcastles with Jesus? What an image! I had not been expecting this, but smiled at where the Holy Spirit was leading me in this session.

"I want you to hear the seagulls cawing, and the roar of the waves crashing. Get into the scene. Bring to mind the unmistakable smell of the ocean. And I want you to see all this writing in the wet sand. Okay? Are you seeing this?"

Her head moved, almost imperceptibly.

"And then, picture a big wave of grace flowing in, washing it all away. Your sins, and those of your co-workers. Gone. The only thing left on the sand is sea foam."

I pictured Jesus on the beach, the ocean spray splattering His white tunic. Some kelp from the last wave had gathered around his wet bare feet—the scars from the nails clearly visible. The image took my breath away.

"Okay. When you're ready to come back into the room, I want you to take a deep breath, and then slowly open your eyes. Feel free to take your time."

Cici's eyelashes fluttered. They had clumped together from tears.

"How was that for you?"

"It was okay. Relaxing. Re-affirming." *Her face certainly looks more peaceful.*

"Did that help you to let go of your frustration with your co-workers?" *Oh, goodness. I sure hope so. Or else I went out on a limb for nothing.*

"Yeah…yeah, it did." I saw a flash of a smile. *So, she can do it!*

"Okay, so when you're at work, and you become frustrated with your co-workers not doing their jobs, or being snarky, or what have you, you can do this same guided meditation. It might help if you can take a quick break—run to the restroom or whatever, and do it there in the ladies' room. Write down all their misdeeds in the sand in your mind, with Jesus right beside you, and watch waves of grace wipe them out to sea."

"All right. I'll do that. Thank you."

"You're very welcome, Cici." *And thank You, Lord.*

Christine Hagion is an ordained minister, counselor, author, and advocate. For over twenty years she has worked with people experiencing family violence, and her work reflects the wisdom she's gained from her clients. Known as "Dr. Red," she seeks to raise awareness about these issues in writing and speaking. www.RevRedPhD.com.

SECOND CHANCES

Jasmine Schmidt

Jess gripped the steering wheel with sheer terror. Her knuckles paled and her fingers began to cramp. Her heart thundered in her ears echoing along with the scattered thoughts in her mind. She stared through the windshield at the house in front of her. There was movement inside and the curtain was pulled to one side as her father peered back at her through the glass. There was no turning back now. He'd seen her.

Jess slowly forced her hands to relax and slip off the wheel. Her hands shook as they collected the car keys and her purse. The driver door felt heavier as Jess pushed it away from her. Her legs threatened to melt beneath her as she slid out of the car. The door thudded closed and Jess stood still, gazing at the house again. He wasn't at the window anymore.

The front door squeaked open, sending her heart into a full sprint. There he was, humor filled green eyes, proud smile lighting up his face, hands outstretched in greeting. He was clueless. Unsuspecting. The next fifteen steps to the door were the hardest steps Jess thought she'd ever taken. She stopped in front of him and tugged up a corner of her mouth into a weak smile.

"H-hello Dad."

"Jess."

To her surprise he wrapped her in a strong hug and laid a kiss in her hair.

"I'm sorry." Jess swallowed. "Dad...there's something I need to tell you." Her stomach dropped as she saw her father's face pale.

"Inside," he said, opening the door for her.

Jess gripped the strap on her purse harder and went into the house. She noticed the blanket on the couch next to the indented pillow. The coffee pot was nearly empty beside his mug on the side table. He had been waiting for her to come home.

The front door shut and her father sank down on the couch. He patted the cushion next to him.

"What do you need to tell me?" His tone was audibly restrained as if he knew bad news was coming.

Jess declined sitting and paced the short length of the sitting room rug, pivoted and then stared at her father. She took a deep breath. Another. Gulped. Opened her mouth and shut it with a firm shake of the head. Jess could feel the tears rushing forward. Her body battled her conscience.

"I'm in big trouble. At least I'm going to be," Jess managed to whisper. "I shouldn't have even been there. I should have walked away. It happened so fast and-and I just went along with it. Oh Dad, I'm such an idiot. Help me. I don't know what to do."

"What happened, Jessica?" Her father leaned forward.

"Carly wanted to TP some lady's house down the block. Mack had all the supplies already and he met us there after dark. We TP-ed the house and Mack got out of control. He disappeared behind the house and when we caught up with him, he'd thrown a rock at one of the windows. Carly followed him through the window saying they just wanted to look around. The alarm went off and Mack came running out threw a bag at me and jumped into his car and sped off. Carly grabbed me and we took off in her car—"

Her father slapped his thigh and stood up. "Are you trying to get yourself thrown back in juvie?"

"No. Dad, I swear, if I'd known what Mack was going to do I would've never been there. I know we shouldn't have TP-ed the lady's house either. Dad, I'm sorry." Jess buried her face in her hands. "I really messed up."

Her father said nothing.

"Please, Dad. You've got to help me. I don't want to go back to juvie. I'll do anything. Please."

"Are you sure there weren't any hidden cameras? No one saw you guys there?" her father questioned.

"I'm sure. Carly checked." Jess nodded, wiping her tears with her hand.

"And you still have the bag?"

"Yeah, it's some really old jewelry. I left it in the car." Jess nawed on her cheek. *Was he really going to help?*

"Good. Then I'll drive you to her house and you can give the jewelry back, make a sincere apology and pray she doesn't press charges. And if there are no charges, I expect you to ask her what you can do to repay her," her father stated firmly.

Jess choked. "But I can't face her. What if she does press charges? Dad, please."

"You can do this or I can drive you down to the station myself."

Jess tightened the slack in her jaw. "Fine."

Her father opened the front door and waited for her to exit. Jess felt herself getting sick as she passed through the doorway. She retrieved the bag from the back of the car and climbed into the passenger seat. Her mind sped in a panic as the car backed out of the driveway. The houses blurred by until the house, covered in toilet paper brought the car to a stop. Seeing the outcome of last night's escapades, only added to Jess's guilt and dread.

"Go on. I'll wait in the car."

Jess nodded, slipping out of the car. She had been wrong before. These were the hardest steps she'd ever taken in her life. When she knocked on the door, the heavy echoes shook her to the core.

"Yes?" The woman smiled at her.

"M-my name is Jessica Calden…" She continued on, explaining what occured the night before, and apologized several times. Hands trembling, Jess held out the bag containing the jewelry.

The woman opened the bag. Tears welled up in her eyes. "Oh, bless you child. These were my grandmother's. Thank you for returning them." The woman pressed the bag to her chest.

Jess blinked. *Bless me?* She wrung her fingers together, not sure what to do next. "I'll understand if you press charges. What we did was wrong and I'm prepared for the consequences. I-I want to make it up to you, whatever you decide."

The woman was silent, studying Jess carefully. She leaned her head to one side. "How old are you, my dear?"

"Sixteen ma'am."

Silence again.

"I believe you understand the severity of what you did…and if I did press charges, the consequences may include juvenile detention."

"Yes ma'am. I'm afraid I'm already acquainted with juvie." Jess gulped. "I don't want to go back."

"I'd like to speak with your parents if that's agreeable," the woman said gently.

"It's just me and my dad."

The woman looked past Jess and waved at her father. Jess didn't need to turn around to know her father had gotten out of the car.

"Ma'am." Her father introduced himself.

"Come inside please. Jessica, why don't you wait out here." The woman spoke directly, inviting her father in.

Jess could only nod, unable to read whether this was good for her case or not. She sat down on the steps as the door shut behind the two of them. Hugging her knees to her chest, Jess waited. Her mind jumped from fear to resignation. She deserved juvie. Her past few years were marred by constant walking on the fine line between right and wrong. She'd been caught before. Months in juvie. Mandatory community service. Required counseling. The courts had warned her of the repercussions another mark on her record would do. If only she hadn't panicked.

The door opened and her father headed down the walkway without a word to her.

"Jessica, I have agreed not to press charges. I will speak with the police and have this matter put to rest," the woman said gently.

Jess couldn't believe her ears. She didn't know whether to cry or celebrate. She wanted to throw her arms around the woman's neck. "Oh, thank you!"

"That's not all. I expect you to clean up this mess," the woman pointed to the strings of toilet paper scattered over the house and yard. "And twice a week you are to come here after school."

"And do what?" Jess asked hesitantly.

"Talk with me, have tea and do your homework. Help me in the yard from time to time. Bake cookies or something." The woman paused. "Does that sound all right to you?"

Jess's eyes widened. *This was too easy.* It even sounded *nice.*

"Yes, I'll be here. Thank you!" Jess couldn't hold back the tears.

"There, there, dear. I don't believe you do these things for pure enjoyment. It seems to me there's a great deal of hurt inside you, you don't know how to express. Some void you can't fill."

Jess sniffled. "I don't understand. Why you are being so nice? I don't deserve your kindness."

"Ah dear. I believe you'd do a great deal better with some extra love and guidance rather than rehabilitation in a detention center. I believe in second chances. It's called grace, Jess. Grace."

*Jasmine writes historical fiction novels for young adults, short stories, and poetry. She has been published in **Inspire Love** and **Inspire Kindness**. Jasmine loves reading and hanging out.*

GRACE IN DEEP DARKNESS

Randy Brundage

In the autumn of 2003, I was committed to a mental hospital. It started with the police pounding on my front door.

The sadness had been mounting for years. About a month before the incident, I reached a critical point. From my bedroom window I listened to a train rumble down the tracks. I contemplated stepping in front of it. *Oh my God, I might really do this!* My eyes popped open with fright. I could feel, almost hear, the hard and rapid thumping of my heart. *But wait. It's okay. The train is two miles away.* My breathing settled and my heart pounded a little lighter. I had a moment of reprieve from the sadness and anxiety. *It could have happened. It might really happen. I might really do this.*

In the days that followed I thought about alternative ways to kill myself. I thought about slitting my wrists. I took a kitchen knife and "practiced" by slicing my arms. There was something comforting about the sharp pain and droplets of blood. It was like I was able to die a little bit at a time, each slice giving me some relief from the emotional pain.

Even before she knew about the cutting, my wife, Tammy, was aware that something was wrong. I remember the confused look on her face when she asked me, "Why would you want to kill yourself? What about me? What about our kids? Don't you love us? Don't you love me?"

I tried to explain that my love for her and our kids was enormous. But the sadness was bigger. Tammy wept. I gazed at her face and saw both aguish and empathy. I sobbed uncontrollably. I thought about the heartbreak I was putting her through. I felt shame because I wasn't strong enough to take care of her. *How could I do this? I hate myself.*

A few days later I was soaking in the bathtub, reading a book, and feeling the warmth of water on my skin. Inside, I felt lukewarm nothingness and cold gloom. Tammy walked in and was startled when she noticed the cuts on my arms. She shook her head slowly and said, "This isn't right, something needs to be done." The next day the police pounded on our front door.

Arriving home from work, I strutted into the house and announced, "Hi, all," to my wife and three teenage kids. My voice was artificially calm and pleasant. I felt like I was the star in a poorly acted sitcom.

Tammy was on the phone and turned away from me. Before she hung up, I heard her whisper, "He's here now."

Then came loud thumps on the front door. My fifteen-year-old son opened the door for the two cops and pointed in my direction. One of them asked, "Does he have a weapon?" My son shook his head. I looked at the men with my arms crossed over my chest and a broad smile on my face. They asked me about my feelings. I told them I felt pretty good. I didn't tell them that I only felt peaceful because I had finally decided to let go of the pain and end my life.

After the brief interview, the police proceeded to leave. Tammy frantically asked, "Why are you leaving without him?"

"He's not that bad, we don't have enough reason to take him."

"But he's planning on killing himself!"

One officer eyed me and asked, "Is this true?"

With a sly smile on my face, I answered, "Well, I wasn't planning on doing anything today. Later, but not today."

He shared a quick look with his partner, then said to me, "Why don't we take you to a safe place where people can help?"

"No, thank you, I'd rather stay home and relax."

Abruptly, his partner grabbed my arms, slammed handcuffs on my wrists, and growled, "Calm down!"

I am calm. What's wrong with you guys? "Tammy, would you tell them they don't have to do this? This is really going to complicate things." I sounded annoyed.

Tammy's eyes were wet and her face was red. Her expression showed regret and relief. She looked away and said nothing.

As they hustled me out the door, I thought, *Why so rough? Relax guys. It's just me.* "This is just like 'Cops,'" I jested, referring to the TV show, "except that I have my shirt on." No one got my joke. As I sat in the backseat of the squad car, I thought, *I hope my neighbors aren't seeing this...so, this is really happening...hey, they forgot to buckle me in!*

Next was a four-hour stopover in a county hospital followed by an ambulance ride to the mental hospital. In the lobby they offered me a beverage. I was pleased when I found out they had cranberry juice. "I'm going to recommend this place to my friends." Again, no one got my joke.

After the first night, I had time to pause and think. I pondered the possibility that maybe God wanted me to die. But If God wanted me to die, He could take me at any time.

He didn't need my help. I shuddered with fright at the thought of God suddenly striking me down...I continued to deliberate. *What if He left me? What if He's gone? What if I'm truly alone?*

For a few moments it felt like I was totally separated from God.

Deep darkness...no light...no hope...alone...without Him...lost.

Fear!

Soon afterwards, my thoughts began to turn around. *I can't trust my feelings. I can only trust the truth. The truth is that Jesus loves me. The truth is that God is with me and will never leave me nor forsake me.* It felt like the Lord wrapped His warm arms around me and said, "Look! See the Light. I am here. Everything will be okay."

That night in my Bible reading I came across Isaiah 60:20:

Your sun will no longer set, nor will your moon wane; for you will have the Lord for an everlasting light, and the days of your mourning will be over. (Isaiah 60:20 NASB)

That passage spoke directly to my heart and mind. It helped me take a step out of my darkness and into the everlasting light. With counseling, medication, and Tammy by my side, the healing continued.

Nine years later, in 2012, Tammy died of cancer. This loss was extremely difficult for our kids and others left behind. The grief of losing my bride and best friend was excruciating for me. I realize now what a horrendous impact my deliberate death would have had on my loved ones. I'm grateful that, by the grace of God, I didn't succumb to the sadness.

Six and a half years after Tammy's death, I can still see evidence of those cuts in the faded scars hiding below the hairs on my arms. I can perceive the deep darkness of 2003 with more clarity. Others go through the joys and trials of life without a close companion. By God's the grace, Tammy was beside me to help along the way. Mental illness often leads to divorce. By God's grace, our marriage survived and thrived. Today, when I have trials from without and struggles from within. When darkness comes my way. I know to look up. I know to look for the Light.

I will lift up my eyes to the mountains; from where shall my help come? My help comes from the Lord, who made heaven and earth. (Psalm 121:1-2 NASB)

Do not fear, for I am with you; Do not anxiously look about you, for I am your God. I will strengthen you, surely, I will help you, Surely, I will uphold you with My righteous right hand. (Isaiah 41:10 NASB)

*Randy is still new to the writing world. He first published in the **Inspire Kindness** anthology. He's been widowed since 2012 and has three adult children who live away from home. He trusts that the Lord will use his story to comfort, encourage, and inspire those who read it.*

GRACE REST

Terrie Hellard-Brown

For it is by grace [God's remarkable compassion and favor drawing you to Christ] that you have been saved [actually delivered from judgment and given eternal life] through faith. And this [salvation] is not of yourselves [not through your own effort], but it is the [undeserved, gracious] gift of God; not as a result of [your] works [nor your attempts to keep the Law], so that no one will [be able to] boast or take credit in any way [for his salvation]. For we are His workmanship [His own master work, a work of art], created in Christ Jesus [reborn from above—spiritually transformed, renewed, ready to be used] for good works, which God prepared [for us] beforehand [taking paths which He set], so that we would walk in them [living the good life which He prearranged and made ready for us]. (Eph. 2:8-10 AMP)

Grace is such a gift, more than we often realize. Grace is what saves us from our sins—pure grace, nothing else, no actions on our part, no duties, no rules, other than accepting God's wonderful grace. But wait, there's more! Grace also releases us from striving and worrying about measuring up to perfection (usually perfectionism in reality). We are free from fear that we are missing out on what God has planned for us. He says it right there in Eph. 2. We are His "workmanship, master work, work of art." And we are created for the good works He has already prepared for us. There's something comforting and restful about those words. As they wash over our minds and hearts, a realization dawns that we are cherished, and we are born with purpose.

"Are you tired? Worn out? Burned out on religion? Come to me. Get away with me and you'll recover your life. I'll show you how to take a real rest. Walk with me and work with me—watch how I do it. Learn the unforced rhythms of grace. I won't lay anything heavy or ill-fitting on you. Keep company with me and you'll learn to live freely and lightly." (Matthew 11:28-20 MSG)

"Learn the unforced rhythms of grace." Those words just make me breathe deeply and relax. So many times, I forget that grace isn't just a salvation thing, it is a living-life-forever-with-our-wonderful-Father-in-Heaven thing. This may not be a major revelation to you. Maybe you've lived your whole Christian life knowing this and simply following God wherever He leads. I, however, have not been that wise.

I am a recovering perfectionist with fear-based tendencies. I walked in striving much more than I walked in grace for many years of my Christian life. I became a Christian at the ripe old age of seven. I was raised to fear many things in life, but the biggest one was failure. I made straight A's, was kind to everyone, and genuinely loved God and wanted to bless others. However, there were no "unforced rhythms of grace" in my mind and heart. There were negative thoughts and fears topped off with criticism by those around me.

Then it happened. I finally truly heard the Word of God. It happened at first in a counseling session when I was a newlywed trying to deal with my husband's brush with cancer. He was fine; the doctors got it all, but I was not fine. I was a mess. Nearly losing him brought every fear to the surface of my life, and I sought the help and wisdom of a wonderful counselor. He began each of our meetings by quoting 2 Timothy 1:7. *For God has not given us a spirit of fear and timidity, but of power, love, and self-discipline.* (NLT) One day he asked me if I thought I was God. Being the "good Christian girl" that I thought I was, frankly, he shocked me with the question. Then he said very simply, "God is the only One who is perfect. Would you agree?" I nodded. "So, when you are striving for perfection through perfectionism, you are trying to be your own God." The realization hit me straight in the face. It was true! I wasn't trusting God. I was trying to be my own God and control everything. As we continued through more meetings, I realized how perfectionism is idolatry and how we deceive ourselves when we think we control much of anything.

Now, one might think this would have thrown me into a tailspin. Acknowledging my lack of control over the world and my serious lack of real perfection should have been devastating. But it wasn't. It opened the door to those "unforced rhythms of grace." It was there all the time. That beautiful, peaceful, joy-filled grace I'd experienced when I was seven was there. And it was meant to be there every moment of my life as I walked with my Savior.

Freedom. True, amazing freedom. That's what I found.

Dear, sweet child of God, are you striving like I did? Are you carrying heavy burdens never meant for your shoulders? Trust God. Receive His daily grace, His resting place, that He has created for us through His mercy and grace.

So then God's choice is not dependent on human will, nor on human effort [the totality of human striving], but on God who

shows mercy [to whomever He chooses—it is His sovereign gift].
(Romans 9:16 AMP)

Father God, thank You for Your grace. Thank You for Your patience with us as we strive so hard to earn the love You have already lavished upon us. Oh, Lord, help us be people of grace who simply walk in obedience and trust with You each day. Open our eyes to Your amazing grace and love, and then, help us to extend it to others. In Jesus' name, amen.

Where are you striving?
What fears are you harboring?
Where do you need to let God's grace come into your life today?

> *Terrie, a California native, grew up in Oklahoma, was a missionary in Taiwan, and has settled in Sacramento. She's a writer, teacher, wife, and mom. But mostly, she's a Christian trying to live her faith. She's been published several times. Favorite topic is Christian life, and she's written children's stories.*

GRACE FOR A FRUITFUL MINISTRY

Christine L'Heureux

"You did not choose me, but I chose you and appointed you that you should go and bear fruit and that your fruit should abide" (John 15:16 ESV).

Where is the fruit? I work so hard but see nothing for my diligent efforts.

As I board the plane to fly back to Japan, I make a final decision. *If the leadership in Japan doesn't allow me to move to a different area, I will quit!*

I've prayed and trusted God to work, but in my heart of hearts, I feel responsible for the outcomes. I feel as if the fruit depends on me. My worth and identity are wrapped up in the results.

I'd been a church planting missionary with OMF International serving in Japan. I loved the Japanese and shared the gospel with them. However, I wasn't seeing the fruit I was looking for; no one I witnessed to believed in Jesus.

Japan has not been very responsive to the gospel. In fact, less than one percent of the population are Christians. The churches are small. Seventy percent of the churches average about thirty members.[1] Missionaries can become discouraged with so little fruit for their labor.

Why is Japan such a difficult place to work?

Many Japanese consider themselves both Buddhist and Shinto. Becoming a Christian is like giving up their culture. How can they stop the Buddhist practice of ancestor worship that shows respect for their dead relatives?

- They believe in many gods, not the one and only Creator God.
- The Japanese concept of sin is committing a crime that shames the family. Personal sin against a holy God is not understood.
- Japanese live by obligation and duty. Faith and grace are not part of the Japanese mind.
- Unless the Holy Spirit breaks through these worldview walls, who can believe in salvation through Jesus Christ alone?

After a year of leading a small church in Aomori City in northern Japan, I was depressed and discouraged. Circumstances were very stressful. Some of the church people and contacts suffered from mental illnesses. I wasn't sure how to support and care for them, but I gave them my listening heart and my time. I loved them but couldn't help them. I felt helpless and powerless.

At the same time, I enjoyed teaching English and studying the Bible with my English students. I also taught the Bible to a group of women—mostly "seekers" who wanted to learn about Christianity. Mrs. Honda[2] was an English student and a "seeker" in the women's group. I spent hours with her trying to convince her that God loved her, and that Jesus died for her

---

[1] Statistics from https://omf.org/asia/japan/resources/about-japan/
[2] Names were changed to protect privacy.

sins. No matter how hard I tried to explain the truth, and even though she diligently studied and tried to understand, she still couldn't believe.

After over six years of ministry as a missionary in Japan, including two years of language study, I had not seen even one person believe in Jesus through my efforts in teaching and evangelism.

I went back to the States for a vacation feeling burned out. I didn't want to continue feeling so useless and discouraged.

While in California, I talked with mission leadership, family, and friends. They all agreed with me that I should move to an easier, more receptive area in Japan. I was relieved and enjoyed the rest of my vacation.

Now, 30,000 feet in the air, we experience the worst turbulence ever. I am so scared. I'm afraid I'm going to die. I feel like Jonah on the ship in the violent storm. He was running away from God's call. Am I also running away?

I realize something that I've overlooked. I had asked family, friends, and mission leadership in the States for their opinion on my *not* going back to Aomori City. I convinced them that I shouldn't go back. They all agreed with me. Somehow, I forgot to ask the Lord what He thought.

I know in my heart almost immediately what the Lord is calling me to do. *Go back to Aomori City.*

I struggle and fight to bring my will to obey His will. I make a commitment to die to myself, my desires, and my plans. I must die to myself, but I can't. The Lord must perform the work. I can't do anything. I see my selfish desires, my lack of love, and my independence of Him. I am more concerned about my comfort than the salvation of the Japanese in Aomori City.

Truly, truly, I say to you, unless a kernel of wheat falls into the earth and dies, it remains alone; but if it dies, it bears much fruit. (John 12:24 ESV)

…apart from me you can do nothing. (John 15:5 ESV)

The fierce battle on the plane is finally over. I'm willing to go back now. I opened my heart to the Lord, and He worked a deep repentance in me. By grace I bear the fruit of repentance—a new dependence on my Lord and surrender to His will. Amazingly, I travel back north to Aomori City with joy.

My circumstances don't change. I continue teaching and spending time with the Japanese. But my attitude is more peaceful and joyful after the battle on the plane and deeper surrender to the Lord. I enjoy my daily times in God's presence and in His Word. I still long for the grace of a fruitful ministry; I desire spiritual children.

One day my English class gathers to watch *The Hiding Place*, the story of Corrie ten Boom and her family rescuing Jews and hiding them in their home during World War II. After Nazis found the hiding place, Corrie and her family were all sent to concentration camps. She was the only one who survived.

I'd invited a new friend, Mrs. Tanaka[2], to join us. As we watch the film, I notice that she is crying. I think maybe the film is touching her heart, but the intensity of emotion seems over-the-top.

After the film, I ask, "Are you okay? Is something wrong?"

She can't answer me. She is still too upset.

A week or two later she shares her heart with me.

"I felt like I was just like the Nazis. I killed my unborn child because having a baby then wasn't convenient."

Abortion is very common in Japan. I once visited a memorial in Tokyo for aborted babies. Toys, bottles, and clothing are placed at these memorial sites. Mothers grieve the loss of their babies.

Mrs. Tanaka needs forgiveness and healing. Her heart is ready to receive both. On Valentine's Day in 1989 at our women's group meeting, Mrs. Tanaka prays with us to receive Christ.

Oh, the joy of her salvation that we experience together! The Holy Spirit fills her with great understanding of the Word. She loves the Lord and His Word, and we enjoy studying together. I am amazed at her growth in grace and in her knowledge of the Lord.

Here is greater fruit than I ever imagined! A spiritual child with a great hunger to know Jesus and to study the Word!

Experiencing the grace of intimacy with the Lord together with spiritual children is indescribable joy. He prepared our hearts. He humbled us and revealed Himself and His love and grace.

Out of all my years as a missionary in Japan, the Lord gave the most fruit in Aomori City. I am so glad that I went back there.

❧

Over 30 years later, I reflect on the lessons learned in Aomori City:

- Abba Father calls us to an impossible task that we cannot complete in our own strength.
- Don't give up. Never give up. The Lord will come and bless.

- The kernel of wheat must fall into the ground and die, or it bears no fruit. We must wholeheartedly surrender to His will and follow Him no matter the cost.
- By God's grace He prepares us to speak the gospel and by His grace people come to know Him.
- *Apart from Me, you can do nothing.* (John 15:5 ESV) He desires intimacy with us and calls us to work with Him.
- In experiencing Him as we work with Him, we see His glory and grace. Jesus becomes our focus, not the fruit.
- Transformation happens when by faith and grace, we take even a baby step of obedience toward Him. He meets us with His love and grace.

Abba Father, thank you for your love and grace. What a delight to work with You. Reveal Yourself to us. Show us where You are working. We will follow You no matter the cost. Amen.

Christine L'Heureux is passionate about knowing Abba Father's heart and sharing His heart with others. She longs to experience a continuing, deeper intimacy with the Holy Trinity. God called her to serve in Japan for about eighteen years to learn and teach the love and grace of God.

INFINITE GRACE

Heather D. Blackman

Grace looked down into time.
Saw my worth,
Took my place,
Sins erased,
Rescued me from my fate.

Grace sees the present.
Embraces me daily
With mercies anew.
Shortcomings known,
Still, my blessings flow.

Grace looked into eternity.
Sealed my future
With God forevermore.
Unearned, undeserved,
My place in Heaven reserved.

Heather D. Blackman

*Heather D. Blackman is honored to share her creative spirit through her passion for writing poetry. Her poems have been published in **Inspire Promise, Inspire Forgiveness, Inspire Joy, Inspire Love,** and **Inspire Kindness**. Heather desires that her poetry will uplift, encourage, and express the love of our Heavenly Father.*

The Holy Spirit's Whisper Becomes Louder, Then Boom!

Charlotte Spink

> *For it is all for your sake, so that as grace extends to more and more people it may increase thanksgiving, to the glory of God.*
> (2 Corinthians 4:15 ESV)

Every year Touchstone Christian Fellowship invites women of all ages and teenage girls to a weekend women's retreat at Zephyr Point Presbyterian Conference Center in Nevada right by Lake Tahoe. This particular year there were over one hundred in attendance. Not all were believers in Jesus Christ as their Savior yet.

On Saturday, October 3, 2015, the Touchstone Christian Fellowship Retreat sessions began with "You Were Created to Flourish in a Garden."[1] Next came "What's So Amazing About Grace Anyway?"[2] Then came the testimony of Brenda Zamorano, and lastly "Awaken in Worship," led by the worship team.[3]

We were invited to take turns coming forward to recite our favorite Bible verse following each worship song that we sang.

---

[1] Presented by Brenda Zamorano, Founder and Biblical Prayer Counselor at Hope In Life Ministry, Sacramento, California

[2] Presented by Melodie Cerrona, Women's Retreat Speaker, Touchstone Christian Fellowship Women's Leadership Team Member

[3] Led by Shirley Bunnell, Worship Team Leader at Touchstone Christian Fellowship, Singer, Song Writer, and Guitar Player.

I was quietly reminded by the Holy Spirit I had received the gift of peace. I truly felt it. Then I was prompted to recite the Twenty-third Psalm. I resisted at first. The Holy Spirit's voice became louder as I was reminded again, "You received peace. Get up there and say the Twenty-third Psalm!" Unbelievably surprised, I went to the podium and began with: "Normally the Twenty-third Psalm is said at funerals. It was pointed out to me that it is about life."

I closed my eyes and recited from memory: "The Lord is my Shepherd; I shall not want. He maketh me to lie down in green pastures: he leadeth me beside still waters. He restoreth my soul: he leadeth me in the paths of righteousness for his name's sake." [4]

Rain began to pound on our roof.

"Yea, though I walk through the valley of the shadow of death, I will fear no evil: for thou art with me; thy rod and thy staff they comfort me. Thou preparest a table before me in the presence of mine enemies: thou anointest my head with oil; my cup runneth over."

Boom! Thunder roared and lightening filled the sky!

My mind went blank. I was in awe and forgot the rest of the verse. When the thunder stopped, the rest of the verse came right back to me. I raised my hands to the sky and shouted:

"Surely goodness and mercy shall follow me all the days of my life: and I shall dwell in the house of the Lord for ever."

We all clapped hands.

I found out later that several women said the Twenty-third Psalm with me and for a couple of them the Twenty-third Psalm came to their minds before I went to the podium. By the grace of God I went to the podium as prompted by the Holy Spirit. Otherwise I would have missed the opportunity

---

[4] Psalm 23 (KJV)

to be the one God chose to show His presence. Everyone was amazed by this event. The next song the Worship Team led was about rain coming down. I am so grateful I did what the Holy Spirit prompted me to say and that I listened to Him. The thunder and lightning were definitely heard and seen in God's timing. They did not occur again throughout the night, only rain showers.

The peace of God overwhelmed me that last night during worship and the joy came with thunder and lightning. Thanksgiving was overflowing among us.

"Time to Advance" by Sharon Miles[5] concluded the retreat on Sunday morning.

Charlotte lives in Rancho Cordova with her feisty cat, Jubilee. She's a beta reader for author Rick Acker, assistant to the Children's Curriculum Coordinator and a prayer team member at Touchstone Christian Fellowship, and memoir writer.

---

[5] Women's Ministry Leader and Children's Curriculum Coordinator for Touchstone Christian Fellowship

Grace Applied

Heather Popish

—⸻◦⸻—

I stood staring into my mailbox, excited yet also disbelieving that it was here. The business size envelope didn't look like anything special, but the return address from our local school district let me know that this was it. After endless months of research, tears, and confusion, I would find out whether or not my daughter was going to be able to start kindergarten that fall in the charter school we had applied to. Desperate prayers had been uttered daily, and I had talked to others until I thought my head would explode from information about all of the options of schooling in our area.

It all culminated into this one moment, my heart pounding as I lifted up the letter. When I grabbed our mail key that evening and headed out into the cool night air, listening to children laughing as they played basketball, I had no idea this would be the day we had our answer. I took a deep breath and started ripping the envelope open.

Years earlier, when my husband and I had bought our first house, the last thing on our mind was what school district we were in. We were so excited to get out of rented apartments, and we found a great house at a good deal. Less than five years later, after having both our children, we were excited, exhausted, and overwhelmed by parenthood. As we started figuring out what

79

we were doing, and our kids grew and we were no longer in that baby haze the thought of their future schooling popped into my mind once in awhile. I assumed it would all work out later when they were older, and so I filed the concern away in my brain. I was in that phase of denial for a while, telling myself we had plenty of time to figure out where they would go to school, and that it probably wasn't a big deal.

One day when I had a few spare moments, I looked up what school district we were in, and which schools we were assigned to, and felt a few moments of panic at the sight of their low ratings. But I still figured that God would lead us where we should go and everything would be all right.

I trusted God in my mind, but had not yet gone through what that meant in a practical way. In order to get from where we were at present, to where we wanted to be in the future, which was having our kids in a good school, there were a lot of steps and pain to go through. I wanted someone to hold my hand every step of the way, tell me what to do next, and what was the right thing to do for our family. I threw panicked prayers heavenward, but mostly felt like I was all alone, trying to keep myself from drowning as I researched schools and options.

As Christians, we say that we believe in God, and trust that He has a plan for us. We know that He loves us, for the Bible tells us so. But how does it look to live that out? How do you go from just saying those words, to really showing with your life that you are leaning on God's promises? It's one thing to say that I won't worry about a certain situation, and will pray for God's leading. But it's a whole different story when deadlines are coming up, paperwork has to be turned in, and I haven't yet heard the voice of God telling me whether I should move to a better school district, or stay where we live and apply to other nearby schools. I was so desperate, thinking maybe I could homeschool (even though I have no patience for teaching and I know my child would miss being around other classmates). Or possibly we'd stumble upon a pot of gold, and be able to send them to a private school.

Decision-making can be such a fine line. I need to bring my prayers and petitions to God, and listen for His leading. But at the same time, I don't think there is a right or wrong answer for every little detail in our lives. We need to use our discernment, which comes to us from God and through praying and reading the Bible, to make these life decisions. Does it really matter which school my child goes to, or is it most important that she is in a school, learning and doing her best, and honoring God wherever she is?

Time marched on during this year of school planning chaos. After much waiting and agonizing, one warm, spring day I walked with my kids down the street to the school that we were technically assigned to. The first official step in this process was to turn in the initial paperwork to this local school. From there we could try to transfer to a different school in the district. There was one that sounded really great, and I was praying with all my might she would get accepted there, but I was also trying not to get my hopes up too much. I was feeling blue despite the beautiful weather, because this huge weight on my shoulders made everything feel hopeless. If she didn't get in to this other "better" school, she could be doomed to a school year full of boredom and possibly falling behind her peers. I walked into the school's office, trying not to cry from despair and exhaustion as I handed the secretary the papers to be photocopied. It took me a few minutes of standing there to get out of the gray cloud in my head, and realize that the song playing on the radio in the office sounded familiar. I only listen to Christian music stations in the car, and recognized this as one of those stations. I couldn't believe they were even allowed to play Christian music on the radio in the office of a public school. It was a small thing, but to me it was clearly a sign from God.

I knew in that moment that everything would be okay. God was speaking to me, and addressing all of my worries and questions. His grace came down and wrapped itself around me in the form of a song from the radio. I didn't hear an audible voice, but I knew God was letting me know that whatever the outcome, to keep leaning on and following Him. That is what is important. If my daughter ended up going to this school, this one that wasn't very well rated, she would be okay. If she got into the charter school that we were going to try to transfer into that has great ratings, she would be okay. Either way, she would learn, grow and thrive, because she is walking with the Lord and He will never leave her side.

Walking out of the school that day, tears streaming down my face, I knew everything would work out, because that's what God promises. *And we know that for those who love God all things work together for good, for those who are called according to his purpose.* (Romans 8:28 ESV) We won't necessarily get what we want, but we can know that whatever happens, God is working it for our good even if we don't fully understand. I learned through this trial just how true that is. I went from praying that she would get into a certain school, or that I would know which decision to make, to instead praying for God to be with me each step of the way, and for Him to continue to pour His grace on me.

I got worried, and I messed up, but He was always with me. God's grace will strengthen me, and my family, as long as we continue to seek a relationship with Him. The other things in life, like schooling, are just details. In light of eternity, this is a non-issue. *My grace is sufficient for you, for my power is made perfect in weakness.* (2 Corinthians 12:9 ESV)

Months later, as I picked that envelope up out of my mailbox, I took a deep breath, feeling like a whole year of trials and tribulations was culminating into that moment. My hands were shaking, and I really wanted to read the news that said my daughter had been accepted into the charter school. But I remembered that day in the school office, and how I felt God was speaking straight to me through that Christian song on the radio. I took another calming breath, and mouthed a thank you to God for His grace towards me throughout this whole process. No matter how big of a mess I feel I make, He never leaves me or gives up on me. I smiled, and returned to ripping open the envelope.

Heather Popish lives with her husband and young children in the Sacramento area. She enjoys being a stay-at-home mom, baking, and encouraging others through her writing.

Transforming Grace

Dian L. Avila

"*Beeeeeeep*," the motion sensor from my mom's room pierced through my dream and peeled my eyes open. My feet pelted every other step of the stairs. My goal was to reach her before she found an exit or a way to hurt herself in the kitchen.

"Good morning, Mom. It's your daughter, Dian," I cued her. She was sitting on her bed.

She pushed aside the walker I placed before her, trying unsuccessfully to get up without it, then grabbed on and lifted herself up.

She asked repeatedly some form of, "Where am I? Do I live here? Is this my house? How long are we staying here?"

"You live here with me now, Mom," I gave my tenth response, as we approached the breakfast table. It hurt to see such an accomplished mind reduced to this. Mom learned to fly an airplane, drew top secret plans during WWII, and raised five children. She was an amazing woman and now, she couldn't remember what I had just told her.

"I'm so glad you could come to Hawaii with us. Look how beautiful it is on the lanai." Her thoughts shifted from the relentless questioning.

My gaze followed hers to our backyard. It was pretty, but it's not Hawaii. I breathed a praise that this morning was Hawaii instead of hallucinations.

Memories of her first months with us darkened my thoughts. I recalled the tense muscles I experienced when she warned me of a strange man on the patio, the insects flying toward my head, or the intruder entering through a window. I felt my heart jump remembering how I flew to her side whenever she tried to rise so I could prevent her fragile body from falling and bruising, which happened easily with the blood thinners she was on.

I snapped out of my gloom to offer her some more coffee. She said, "Thank you. You are so nice. You remind me of my daughter Dian. She's pretty. You even look a lot like her." I didn't correct her. I don't remember her calling me pretty to my face much when I was growing up. She was always kind, but she probably thought such compliments would inflate my ego. There were other things this dementia called Lewy Bodies said and did through her that would have humiliated her. But one good thing was she didn't remember how this frontal lobe brain disease distorted her thoughts and actions. Sometimes it even caused aggressive behavior or hysterical screaming caused by an irrational fear. Both behaviors were so opposed to her docile, courageous, intelligent, and kind personality. I began cleaning up the dishes.

"Can I help you, sweetie?" Mom tried to rise.

"No, it'll just take me a second. Would you like to play some cards? Here, you can deal them out." I handed her a Canasta deck knowing the game we played would only slightly resemble Canasta.

Mom began one of my favorite stories, "Did I ever tell you about our pet duck, Bitty, the neighbors teased us about? She used to follow us to school and the children would laugh at us for having a pet duck. You know why they teased us? It was the Great Depression and everyone thought the duck should be dinner." I had heard the story multiple times, but never the last part. I thought it was hilarious and wondered why she always left that part out.

I began thinking again of those difficult first days as her caregiver. Every trip to the ER, and there were many, wore me out with my worries. Those days, my nerves were tighter than last decade's jeans and my heart raced like I was in a marathon. One night, in the beginning of her fourth month with us, she refused to stay in bed for the second night in a row. It wasn't like we got much sleep anyway with her night wandering and delusions, but she hadn't even taken a ten-minute nap in more than 80 hours.

Sometime after midnight, I dragged myself upstairs, hoping she would spend some time quietly rearranging her books, packing a suitcase or just walk around her room reliving some day long gone so I could get at least an hour nap. I immediately drifted into a delightful, deep sleep. Twenty minutes later, screaming rattled the monitor.

My head was a boulder on my pillow. My eyes were glued shut. I hesitated, waiting to see if the screaming would stop, but she sounded genuinely hurt this time. My feet felt their way down the steps; my eyes tried to focus now and then to check my progress. The sleep fog in my brain was massive. Seeing my mom on the floor moaning with the bed covers wrapped around her legs penetrated the fog. My worse fear was realized when the X-rays confirmed she had broken her neck. This prognosis increased the complexity of her care. We had to make sure she kept the brace on her neck as well as keeping her from falling or leaving the house. The term 24/7 took on a whole new meaning as I took up residence on the floor of her room. We installed a motion sensor that she usually ignored, but sometimes played with by waving her hand above her bed to make it beep repeatedly. I laugh at that now, but at the time when I was sleep deprived, I found it anything but funny.

She broke her neck over a year ago. I thought I had been relying on the strength of our Lord previously, but that night, He drew me under His wings and into His presence. I realized I had been an anxious mess before my mom broke her neck fearing that she would, well, break her neck. I had been entreating Jesus on her behalf and asking for guidance to be His love to her, but I hadn't really given Him my fears. I had read, quoted, and prayed, *"Casting all your anxieties on him, because he cares for you,"* (1 Peter 5:7 ESV) multiple times, but now I finally lived it. Whenever an anxious thought crept into my brain, I captured it and let Jesus replace it with His peace. It became a joy to spend time with my mom, finding blessings in each manifestation of the horrific disease called Lewy Bodies which was a feat only accomplished with divine power. God was working on me, giving me reliance on Him and patience only the Holy Spirit and grace can give.

I marveled at her hallucinations instead of shrinking from them. When I confessed I could not see what she was seeing, she got excited and began describing exactly what the feathered, blue horse was doing on the fence in the backyard. I still rose when she rose to prevent falls, but with patience and gratitude for the opportunity to reciprocate the care she had given me. And when I heard that childhood or war story for the 123rd time, I was inspired, listening to her relive it as if it were yesterday or we were in the moment like finding out Bitty should have been supper. There was more emotion and detail when she related life from her childlike brain. So now, whether or not my alarm, her motion sensor, coincides with the rising sun, I give thanks.

I was transformed into a more trusting, patient, and peaceful person by God's grace while caring for my mom in her suffering. Learning to redirect tantrums, meltdowns, and moments when she was terrified at invisible threats was beyond difficult on my own, but with God's grace, I was able to meet her needs. Eventually she needed more care than I could give and I moved her to a facility where she lived on hospice for two years. By God's provision and grace, it was down the street from my home and I could walk to her new place to visit and still spent time with her every day. I am who I am because she is part of me. She was able to teach and inspire me even in her last years when she wasn't truly herself. Praise God for His generous grace.

Dian lives in South San Jose, CA with her husband, Jose and adult son, Daniel. She and her husband are missionaries in Latin America. Dian is also the Dean of Students at Legacy Christian School.

THANK GOD

Delores Vavrinec

"You are My servant, I have chosen you and not rejected you. Do not fear, for I am with you; do not anxiously look about you, for I am your God. I will strengthen you, surely I will help you, surely I will uphold you with My righteous right hand."
(Isaiah 41:9-10 NASB)

God gave me this scripture when I was crying out of desperation because I was spiritually empty. Looking for Him in the ceiling and in the wall from my hospital bed. I tried to call Denise, my pastor's wife, but I couldn't reach her and then I realized God wanted me to find Him in me. A Christian nurse came in and began to talk to me about her walk, about how she had brought all her family to Christ. I began to tell her how important it was to read the Word. She said, "It looks like you have a real nice Bible there." It was lying on my side table by my bed open.

Oddly enough it was open to Isaiah and when she left I began to read: *I said you are my servant.* It was already highlighted in yellow. I had no memory of doing it. I continued reading through the tenth verse. I soaked it in; it said exactly what I needed to hear. God wanted me. He wasn't going to throw me away. He had even chosen me and I was to work for Him. He did not reject me. My body was rejecting me but God was not. I am not to be afraid for He is with me. He will strengthen me and I was weak and I had renewed hope in receiving strength. My body was at its lowest. He will help me and I needed His help so bad plus He will hold me up with His righteous right hand. Imagine He's going to hold me up not with anything less than with His righteous right hand. This is the Holy God of the Universe.

How did I find this Scripture? The Bible was already open to it and it was colored with my yellow marker. I didn't remember it. I had no knowledge of highlighting it.

That Scripture, when she left the room, leapt off the page to me. I read it over and over: it sustained me throughout my recuperation from pancreatic surgery and kidney failure, but after a couple years, Bible studies and other ministries covered it up and I began to forget about Isaiah 41. I joined a prayer group. There were twelve of us meeting on a regular basis at Virginia's. Peggy Berry was leading and she assigned each of us a Scripture. And mine was Isaiah 41:9-10. God was reminding me once again. Twelve people, twelve verses, and I got that one. No accident. God reminding me I belong to Him.

Now recuperating from thyroid surgery and adverse reactions to medications, I read Isaiah 41:9b-10 and it ministers to my heart and soul. Don't let go of me, God, I am nothing without you!

Delores has written for years but has not been published.

Unexpected Grace

E. V. Sparrow

Grimy salt water sloshed up through the wooden floorboards of the ferry loaded with vehicles and taxis. The ferry dipped and swayed as it cast off from a jetty on the Suez Canal's east bank. Lauren leaned out the taxi's rear side window and gripped the sill as three inches of water rose along the tires. She spun to her friend, Dahlia, wedged tight between their backpacks. "We'll sink!"

"Sink? I can't see a thing."

"I've never seen a ferry like this. It's a raft with an engine...a taxi float."

Dahlia craned her neck for a better view. "It's the only way to cross the Suez Canal."

"I didn't want to go to Egypt." Lauren gazed at the water's surface surrounding them. "The Israelis warned us."

"We discussed this back on the kibbutz. Flying out of Tel Aviv to Munich was three hundred dollars more than airfare from Cairo."

Lauren folded her arms. "It had better be worth the savings."

The women disembarked and stood in a long line of travelers waiting at the Sinai-Egyptian border crossing. Perspiration trickled down Lauren's back in the late afternoon heat. She gulped water from her insulated canteen. "What's happening?" She rose on her tiptoes.

"I'll go look." Dahlia leaned her backpack against Lauren's. She scurried down the line and out of sight. Dahlia returned, "It's not good. The border guard is harassing a Hasidic Jewish family. He won't let them cross."

"Isn't there peace with Israel now? President Reagan said something about that."

"No, silly, you're thinking of the ceasefire between Israel and Lebanon, three months ago. Egypt's been okay, but something's up with the guard."

Frantic male voices rose, and people in line jostled each other. A lady near Lauren mumbled, "Do what the guard tells you."

Rejected, the terrified Jewish parents rushed their children back to the border entrance.

Lord, comfort that family.

Lauren and Dahlia waited several uncomfortable hours to hand over their passports and plop their backpacks on the counter to be searched. A young guard unzipped the packs. Lauren's heart pounded. *Lord, help us get through.*

"Your passports have Israeli stamps in them!" The older guard shoved them in the women's faces. "Why would you go there?" He snarled and spit on the cement.

Lord, I'm scared. Lauren glanced at the frightened people in line behind them. *Protect us.*

"We are tourists." Dahlia smiled at the younger guard.

Lauren glanced at Dahlia. *I hope that's all he asks.*

The guards seized the women's cameras from their packs, yanked out the film, and threw it on the concrete. People gasped. The guard sneered, "Too bad, you will not have those photos of Israel." Lauren stared at her feet. *Lord, deliver us from evil.* The guards grabbed their water canteens and emptied them onto the cement. *Lord, restrain violence.* The crowd murmured.

"What?" The older guard taunted, "Do you care we spilled out Israeli water? Do you wish to fight?" No one spoke. He sniggered and shoved the backpacks at the women. "Here, I feel nice this evening. Go."

Lauren and Dahlia swung their packs onto their backs. They scuttled away from the guards until the concrete slab ended on the open desert where taxis waited for travelers. The golden hues of the desert turned blue and purple with the sunset on the vast horizon. Lauren raised her brows. "Dahlia, I prayed so hard."

"I did, too. If he found out we worked on an Israeli kibbutz, he would have freaked, right?"

"Yeah."

"Hey, there's only three taxis, let's grab one." Dahlia detained a driver and asked if he had room. The other two taxis left, full of passengers. Dahlia bickered with the driver as he loaded their packs into the trunk that had no lid. "We know the rate is three pounds."

The driver bellowed. He jerked their backpacks out of the trunk and flung them on the ground. He climbed into his taxi, slammed the door, and drove away in a dust cloud.

Lauren stared. "*Huh?* He left us here?"

"I'm sorry," Dahlia's voice trembled.

Lauren turned toward the border entrance. Cyclone fence, razor wire wound on top, and a locked gate. "We're stuck here!" She panted, "Empty buildings. No lights anywhere. No water." The first stars twinkled in the nightfall.

"And it's getting dark." Dahlia laid her backpack near her feet.

"Don't scorpions and snakes come out at night?" Lauren scanned the area in the twilight. Insects hummed around them. *Lord, help us.* "What do we do?" From a distance, people were shouting. "Do you hear that?"

"Where's it coming from?" Dahlia twirled around. "There." She pointed toward the gloomy horizon.

"I can't see." The noise drew closer. "The taxi." Lauren squealed and hopped with glee. "He came back! The passengers are yelling." The taxi skidded to the slab. The driver rushed out, grabbed their packs, and threw them into the open trunk. He snarled something and climbed inside.

"Get in…" Dahlia climbed onto her pack stuffed in the trunk, and Lauren followed. "We're riding in the open trunk… this would never pass in America." The taxi sped off. The rear window glass missing above the trunk made it easier to haul passengers like cargo. "It's a five-hour drive to Cairo. Hang on tight, or we'll bounce out without our packs."

Lauren looped her arm around the window frame. "Unbelievable." She was glad she was short, because the roof of the taxi shielded her from the sand and dust blowing past. "I hope the others don't mind we're sitting on their luggage. Thank God the driver came back."

The young woman sitting in front of Lauren twisted around. An infant slept against her chest. "We told him he could not leave you there, and we would report him if he didn't return for you. That should not happen, even to people who like Israel."

"You heard that border guard?"

"We all did. We don't want our country to treat tourists badly. My name is Safiya. I am a doctor of women's health."

The balding man next to Safiya smiled. "I am Ahmed, a professor at university." The other passengers made their introductions. The women thanked the friendly group, but the taxi driver scowled in his rearview mirror.

An occasional building, a lone light, and then small villages appeared in the desert night. All the passengers were asleep, except Lauren. *Wish I could sleep. I'm too thirsty.* The taxi bumped along a dirt road, parked in front of a low building, and the driver stepped out. *Maybe he'll bring us some water.* Lauren kept time on her wristwatch. He returned in about fifteen minutes and drove on. He stopped at two more villages. Lauren shook Dahlia awake. "He keeps stopping at houses in every village. It'll take forever to get to Cairo."

Safiya yawned. "He will stop to visit his relatives. His cousin, then his uncle, now his brother."

"What did he mumble at the first stop?"

"He warned us he would take his time. He punishes us for our threats, but you are worth it." The other passengers stirred and agreed.

Seven hours later, at 2:00 am, they arrived in Cairo. Lauren stared at the throng. "Why is it so crowded?"

"The heat of the day is harsh." Safiya explained, "They do business at night."

Horns blew, and drivers shouted out their windows. No one used blinkers, stoplights, or crosswalks. Vehicles swirled every direction between pedestrians and Bedouins on camels or donkeys. Lauren squealed and squeezed her eyes shut. Dahlia shrieked, "They honk instead of using blinkers!" The Egyptian passengers laughed. One by one, the driver delivered them to their destinations in Cairo. He parked near a three-story dilapidated building with no windows and jerked his head at Lauren and Dahlia. The driver unloaded their packs and left the women on the sidewalk. "This is a Four-Star Hotel?" Dahlia complained.

Lauren peered through the empty doorjamb. "Maybe back in 1939?"

"It might collapse. Oh, look, a caged-in elevator."

Lauren inspected the gate. "It's locked." They climbed the winding marble stairway to the lobby. Backpackers were strewn asleep across the tiled floor. The women approached the concierge behind a desk.

"English?" His dark eyes twinkled. "Tired?"

Dahlia sighed. "We've had an awful day."

"The border guards poured out our water," Lauren whispered. "Now, this…sleeping on the floor?" She gulped back tears. Dahlia squeezed her shoulder.

"*Ah*, sad day. Drink bottled water—is safe." He reached under the counter. "Here."

"Hallelujah!" Lauren snatched the offered bottle and opened it. "Thank you. We haven't had water in forever…" Both Lauren and Dahlia gulped their entire bottles.

The Concierge grinned. "I know that word—hallelujah. Christians, yes? I too, believe. Take free room." He slid a key across his desk.

"Why free?" Dahlia frowned.

"Because Scripture says do good to all men, especially to those in the household of God." The Concierge pointed, "You are my sisters."

Writer and illustrator, E.V. Sparrow, served on mission trips, a worship team, and as a prayer ministry leader. She volunteered with Global Media Outreach, at Serna Village, and led small groups in single's, women's, and divorce care ministries. Sparrow's published short stories encounter the unexpected.

MUSIC SPEAKS

Ellen Cardwell

―⚬⚬⚭⚬⚬―

"…singing and making melody in your heart to the Lord,"
(Ephesians 5:19b NKJV)

Do you wake up with a song in your heart? I frequently do, and most of the time the tune is one of the praise choruses we sing at church. It happens so often I think little of it, and the song fades away as the busyness of life presses in.

However, I've discovered that if I'll sing a few phrases, even if I don't know all the words, it builds me up and sets the tone for that day. Then it returns from time to time, refreshing me.

Occasionally, a song grips my attention longer than usual. When that happens, I've learned to listen to the lyrics, because the words are a message to my heart. It may pertain to a situation I'll encounter later that day, helping me handle it wisely. Or, it may address a worry on my mind and diminish the size of the concern, reminding me that God is bigger than my problem.

Not long ago, I bemoaned the fact I'm not physically able to do more—no ministry, fewer commitments, and no responsibilities at church. In fact, I was so tired I lay down for a nap. When I awoke, God answered me with an idea using the song, "All I Ask of You" from *Phantom of the Opera*. He wants me to love Him and that's all He asks. I relaxed into His grace, ever so grateful for His comfort.

God knows how to communicate with each one of us best, be it through preaching or teaching, through reading His word, or through the vehicle of our particular gifts. That He speaks to us through music is a beautiful thing.

Next time a song comes to mind, listen carefully. It could be God's grace notes sent to you for that day.

Ellen's fondness for books began with children's classics and developed through many visits to the library, where she later worked during her school years. Eventually, she penned notes, wrote newsletters, and created ad copy, all of which segued into writing professionally. Inspirational and non-fiction articles are among her published works.

GOD DIRECTS ME THROUGH FIRST TIME HOME BUYING

Charlotte Spink

> *But grace was given to each one of us according to the measure of Christ's gift.* (Ephesians 4:7 ESV)

While life speeds on, you may hear a whisper of great advice giving you a new direction. Will you heed it or ignore it? Does it contradict God's Word? I listened. Here is what happened.

The Whisper of Advice from the Holy Spirit

One day in 1989, much to my surprise, I heard a whisper of advice. *Now is the time to buy your house.* I believe by the grace of God it came from the Holy Spirit.

I attended a First-Time Homebuyers Seminar at North American Title. Afterward I met with real estate broker Harry Guadio at Artz & Cook to begin the process. Harry was my friend Martha's husband and was the top guy at Artz & Cook at the time. He became the real estate broker for my purchase. I made an offer on a house in Rancho Cordova. I accepted the counteroffer on June 10. I moved in sometime around the end of August or early September. EGH and JEF and Rick

Kozlowski helped me move. I borrowed a truck from Lanny K., who had to work that day.

Unknowingly I Describe the Home I Would Buy

My real estate agent took me to at least three ugly homes in my price range. Then I told her I wanted a home that would be near a light rail station along Folsom Boulevard. That way I wouldn't have to drive downtown to work. She found one in Rancho Cordova. It was walking distance from a good friend's house too. Although a light rail station was not within walking distance yet, it would be soon. The current station at Bradshaw Road had a nice parking lot for my car. While the agent was driving me to the house in Rancho Cordova, I told her I wanted a gray house with blue trim, two-car garage, three bedrooms, two bathrooms, fireplace, and brown wall-to-wall carpeting. She drove up to it. There it was: a gray house with blue trim. When I walked in and saw the carpeting along with everything else I requested, I said, "This is it." What a surprise. I believe my description of this house was directed by the Holy Spirit through me. I had no advance knowledge about it and gave it no prior thought.

Unfortunately Jealousy Broke Apart
A Long-Time Friendship

The saddest thing about this purchase is that EGH told me she was very jealous of me because I was buying a home. From that point on I did not tell her all that the Lord was giving me. She hurt me too much. I hoped she would be happy for me. I had shared so much with her for several years. Now I couldn't speak with her about anything having to do with the purchase of my first house. I am so sorry she missed out because, by the grace of God, the Lord advised me the entire way.

God's Further Guidance

During the process, He told me to go ahead and apply for a Mortgage Income Credit (MIC) for first-time home buyers. The application cost two hundred fifty dollars. I was told I had a ninety-nine percent chance I would *not* get my application approved. Another whisper: *Go ahead, apply*. I applied. Later the mortgage company representative told me my application was approved faster than any she had ever seen.

Guilty Feeling Removed

I was feeling somewhat guilty for taking the down payment from Mom's funds. God took care of that too. Mom always wanted me to buy a house with my inheritance, but now was the time. She was still alive. I had her power of attorney and was her conservator/executor. The mortgage lender said I had to have something in writing from Mom approving the monetary gift she was giving me. What a blessing. I wrote up a permission sheet for her approval and signature and the signature of a witness. Mom was in a nursing home in Tennessee. I called a friend of the family back there. He agreed to explain the situation to Mom and ask her to sign the permission sheet. She agreed. No more guilt. By the way, Mom never ran out of money during her lifetime and was still able to give me a nice inheritance.

Where God's Portion of Excess Escrow Funds to Be Spent

I became a first-time home owner on July 19, 1989. Yes, in 1989 God told me it was time to buy my first house. I followed His urging. I prayed each and every step of the way.

Toward the end of the process, when the money was in escrow, I prayed that I would get a six-thousand-dollar refund, three thousand for God and three thousand for me. I was at work when the call came in, sitting at my desk with no one else around. The refund was a little over six thousand dollars. Tears of joy streamed down my face. I was truly *blessed again*. And that's not all. Within a few years housing prices skyrocketed upward and then dropped. Had I waited, I very likely would have ended up "under water" like so many people did.

God's three thousand dollars was used to help EGH's teenager get braces and pay for his high school extracurricular activities like yearbooks, clothes to wear at dances and entrance fees, our church's children summer camps, and more. Somehow the three thousand dollars lasted four years until graduation. I told his mother and him where the money came from, but I don't know whether they really understood that it was not my money. Yes. By the grace of God I was able to put aside my hurt and do what God told me to do with His money.

God's grace is overwhelming. Listen. Pray.

Charlotte lives in Rancho Cordova with her feisty cat, Jubilee. She's a beta reader for author Rick Acker, assistant to the Children's Curriculum Coordinator and a prayer team member at Touchstone Christian Fellowship, and memoir writer.

102

Out of the Weeds

Beth Miller Cantrell

Drinking in the fragrance of an early morning rain, Bob sipped his hot drink and thanked the Lord for another day—a gift from the Creator. Beth, his wife, sat down beside him, and they watched the sunrise. It was special to see the glow and the promise of a sunny day following three days of off and on hard rain.

Looking at her watch Beth said, "This is so peaceful, but it's time to go to the gym."

In the car, the sun was not to be found, for a light sprinkle came as they looked to the west. Then heavy, giant droplets fell which needed the windshield wipers. In front of the clouds a wide strip appeared in brilliant rainbow colors. By the time they arrived, the rainbow had disappeared into more dark clouds, but still, the vision kept a hopeful spot in their hearts.

After their water aerobics class, Bob waited for his wife outside, in an effort to capture some fleeting sun rays that now peeked between the clouds.

A woman came up to Bob. "I see you're enjoying the prospects of a bright day." They carried on small talk about the gym and the exercises.

"By the way, I'm Bob. My wife and I joined the gym water aerobics class. The walking forward and backward in the water has definitely made my legs stronger." Bob gave a little tap dance holding onto his cane to prove his new agility.

The woman laughed. "I'm Cheryl, and my body overall is stronger and better because of the weight lifting I do here. Say what are you and your wife doing this afternoon?"

Bob replied without hesitation, "I'm going home to pull weeds, but first I'm going to eat and rest after all the exercise this morning."

Cheryl tipped her head to the side. "Would you like some help with the weeding?"

Taking off his cap and rubbing his head, Bob replied, "Well, yes, I guess so. I never thought about that. Why would you want to pull my weeds? It's work."

Cheryl smiled. "Maybe that's why. It's work that gets put off, but could use company to get done. Besides, our church has been encouraging us to be like the Good Samaritan—to see a need and try and fill it. Since I'm forty-three and you must be double my age, I would like to help make your project a little easier."

Bob smiled. "You're right; I'm eighty-nine years old. The best I can do is the basics of what needs to be done, but your help would be very nice. My wife has stiff knees that don't bend well, so she leaves the weeding to me. She does inside jobs. When I was young, I used to be the one who helped others, but now my lower energy and lower strength has limited my ability to be there for others."

"Bob, you don't need to be apologizing that you can't do what you did when you were younger." Cheryl gave Bob a thumbs up sign. "Don't you realize most people your age are either in their recliners at home or in recliners at old folk's homes? You're an all-star home maintenance man—if you do even half of the things I suspect you do. Don't tell me you trim your own bushes, too?"

Bob chuckled, "Well all I can say is, you won't find me sitting in my recliner if there's something I'm able to do outside."

Bob shuffled around on his cane and saw his wife had come out of the gym. "Honey, I'd like you to meet Cheryl. She has graciously offered to help me pull weeds."

Beth's eyebrows lifted as she scooted her walker closer to Cheryl. "Wow! How nice to meet you and how great of you to volunteer. Are you sure you want to do some weeding?"

"Well, I'm willing to work at it today and see how it goes. How about I come over about 1:30?" Cheryl put out her hand to shake. "It would give me joy to do weeding for you as I believe we all would benefit."

True to her word, Cheryl appeared on Bob and Beth's front yard. "Time to get to work," she said as she crouched down next to a patch of weeds.

"Would you like to start around the stump? The property managers took that twenty-five-foot tree out, two years ago. I miss it—at least I miss the shade but not mess. First the spring blossoms floated down, then the seed pods, and in the fall all the leaves and twigs came off with every breeze or just because they were ready to let loose."

Having looked up to where the tree had been, Bob shifted his attention and his spade hit a rock. His hand slipped and was cut by the sharp tool. It sliced across his palm, leaving an ugly gash. Bob's face turned pale—ashen gray, in contrast to the bright red blood streaks that dribbled on the weeds and mingled with the earth. He protected his hand to avoid the dirt and squeezed it to blood wash his wound.

Cheryl called into the house for Beth. Together they helped Bob up the mobile stairs and into the bathroom. The cool water soon swept clean the cut area.

"Don't worry about me; I'm covered by His blood." Bob raised his hand to examine the depth of the cut. "Come lay your hands on my arm and let's pray." They gave God the glory for being the healer and especially for healing Bob's palm.

Bob gained back some face color. "It's better now, the bleeding has stopped."

"Let's do our part." Beth reached for the antibiotic. After the dressing was completed, Bob relaxed in his recliner. His palm pulsated less under the butterfly bandage and the sting of the cut.

Cheryl waited until Bob drifted off to sleep and returned to weeding. Soon she decided to call it a day. She put the tools away, said good-bye to Beth with the promise of returning, and drove away. "I'll be back, for there is more to do."

"Thanks so much for being here and helping." Beth smiled. "You have blessed us."

⁓◌∞◌⁓

A week later, Bob sat on his porch in his rocking chair enjoying the sunshine, and saw Cheryl drive up. He waved and called out to her. "Good to see you. Are you interested in pulling more weeds?"

"Yes, I've brought some tools and have come back to weed. Are you up to it?" She walked to the porch. "I haven't seen you at the gym and wanted to check on you."

"The infection of the past week was better kept out of the water." Bob gingerly went down the porch steps. "I've been home for a time but am ready to work now if I could be any good one-handed. I'm willing to give it a try." He pulled his straw hat over his forehead.

The two sat on the front lawn pulling dandelions with Cheryl's tools. Bob worked his right hand and rested his left on his lap.

Beth came around the house with a twenty-gallon trash bag and some cold-water bottles. She helped put rake-full batches of weeds into the bag. Then they sat on lawn chairs and took a break drinking the water. Cheryl and Bob had diligently tugged the weeds for more than an hour, all the time sharing about the healing grace of Jesus. They sat basking in the presence of His favored peace.

"How is the hand tenderness feeling now?" Beth asked.

Bob took off the bandage from his palm. He opened and closed his fist several times without any grimace for pain. "It's doing well. It has closed up and the redness is gone. Praise God for His healing favor. I'm thankful."

Clasping her hands around her water bottle Cheryl said, "That's good, you are blessed. He cares about all our pains."

Cheryl looked up to the sunny sky and noticed the gutter that ran along the porch roof. "Look, more weeds to pull! See those green stems and leaves hanging over the gutter?"

"We've seen them for a year but not been able to get on a ladder to clean them out," Bob murmured.

"Well, I can get them. I'll bring a ladder just the right size to reach. I'll do it, but for now, I need to go home to fix supper."

The next sunny day, Cheryl appeared with her ladder on top of her van. One-handed Bob dragged over the watering hose. Bob helped lean the ladder firmly on the ground and soon hardened weeds and dirt clumps turned to mud poured down. It was slow going until the property manager came by, saw their effort, and came back with a curved ending for the hose, which doubled the proficiency of the water pressure. It took a time and they were wet from the splashing, but the job was done and there was delight at their finished work.

After Cheryl left, Beth and Bob sat on their porch in their rocking chairs, again enjoying the last moments of twilight. Beth turned to Bob saying, "What a gift Cheryl has been."

Bob nodded taking Beth's hand in his. "Grace is what I'd call it. God's favor."

Beth Miller Cantrell is a continuing member of Inspire Christian Writers since its inception. She served on the Inspire Board for ten years and now facilitates the Vacaville critique group. Beth has published two books and appeared in eight anthologies. She lives with her husband in Northern California.

GRACE UPON GRACE: OR PASS THE POTATOES

Tessa Burns

Are you the type of person who designates holidays as guilt-free eating? You don't worry about calories. You just enjoy the yummy feast set before you with no other thought but the explosion of flavor as your taste buds come to life. Happily, you slap that second helping of mashed potatoes on your plate. The slab of butter overflows as it melts down from the top of your potato volcano, dripping down golden sunshine. Oh, the joy!

May I respectfully suggest this is a picture of grace. The unmerited favor of God. Humankind has a sin debt. It is a spiritual genetic condition we are all born with, and there is nothing we individually or corporately can do to fix it. But that is exactly where grace comes in. *For by grace you have been saved through faith. And this is not your own doing; it is the gift of God...* (Romans 6:14 ESV). God has given us the gift of His Son. In His holiness and by His grace He sent Jesus as the propitiation of our sin. Propitiation—try to say that three times fast! What a word. Propitiation is an action to regain someone's favor, to make up for something done wrong, to appease. Jesus was given for our propitiation. *We are justified by His grace as a gift, through the redemption that is in Christ Jesus, whom God put forward as a propitiation by His blood, to be received by faith. This was to show God's righteousness because in His divine forbearance He had passed over former sins.* (Romans 3:24, 25 ESV). 1 John 2:2 says He did not just pass over my sin, or yours, but over the whole world's. Jesus bought our favor back when He offered Himself as the sacrifice for our sin. Can you imagine? Our debt is paid! In full! No calories to count when it comes to our sin. It's the holiday! It is a Holy Day we can rejoice in; the day each of us takes that step and receives the gift of grace that God offers us through His Son Jesus Christ. We no longer need to live in guilt, bound by a sinful nature. Our old congenital spiritual condition is gone, our new congenital condition has come (2 Corinthians 5:17—the old has passed away, and the new has come). We can now walk in the freedom and blessing that grace provides.

Blessed is the one whose transgression is forgiven; whose sin is covered. Blessed is the man against whom the Lord counts no iniquity, and in whose spirit there is no deceit. (Psalm 32:1,2 ESV). We are made clean and new by receiving the gift of grace offered us. And it's not just one serving. John 1:16 (ESV) says, *For from His fullness we have all received grace upon grace.*

So, pass the potatoes. Pass the butter. It's the holiday! And it's time to celebrate!

Tessa lives in Sonoma County with her husband and has three grown children. Her heart is to encourage others to notice and recognize the love God has for them and the beauty that He has created for us to enjoy.

GOD'S TRUTH BY HIS GRACE

Dian L. Avila

I am redeemed, reconciled by Christ,
Forgiven for always for Christ,
Forever a friend to Jesus,
And I am living in His eternal realm.

I am a chosen child of my God,
God's workmanship, made to bear fruit,
Safely sealed by Holy Spirit,
And I am enough because in me Christ lives.

I am adored, admired, not abandoned,
God's. Pure, purposeful, protected,
Resting in Jesus' mild yoke,
And I am blessed, content, at peace, and grateful.

I am invited by Jesus to learn,
Not separated from His love,
Given a spirit of power;
There is no fear, just love and belonging.

I live loved by my King, Daddy, Friend, God,
Transformed to be like my Jesus,
I am filled to God's full measure,
And I rejoice in Christ my King at all times.

Dian lives in South San Jose, CA with her husband, Jose and adult son, Daniel. She and her husband are missionaries in Latin America. Dian is also the Dean of Students at Legacy Christian School.

From the Grave to His Grace

Ian Feavearyear

The boy watches himself in his own grave. Through a cross-section of the earth, he sees himself lying in his coffin, wearing the gray shorts, long gray socks, shirt, sweater, and dress shoes he wears to school. *Why school clothes?* He sees a house, people going in and out, kids laughing, a mother going about her business. All of them oblivious to the seven-year-old lying there. Dead. Underground. Where no-one sees him. Forgotten.

What's the point? Surely there's more to life than this...isn't there?

The summer of the year I entered adulthood will forever be known as "that long hot summer." The three-or-so months between graduating my local community college and starting my degree at university were a long sequence of lazy days spent walking in the woods and fields, hanging out with my lifelong friend, Julie, and my college friend, Mark. Though they weren't all lazy. Mark and I also worked for two to three weeks at a local orchard. Tiresome, tedious work. But at least we got to earn a few pounds while listening to BBC Radio One. And sometimes, just sometimes, we did something crazily spontaneous—like the late night drive to the coast, just because we could.

Julie, whom I'd known since starting school at four, introduced me to so many things I loved: Elvis, Don McLean, Susan Polis Schutz. She called herself a Christian, though she rarely went to church. Mark also claimed to be a Christian and occasionally attended his local Anglican church. I suspected it was his refuge from an abusive father. At least I guessed it was. I knew Mark slept with a knife under his pillow, was very protective of his mother, and never let me visit him at his house.

Mark was the only one of us who could drive and had a car. Perhaps it was because of this that Julie asked me and Mark if we'd like to go with her to a small, local, Baptist church, in the nearby village of Horham. Mark would have done anything for her, and I just wanted to be with them, so, of course, we both said, "Yes!"

I'd attended the children's Sunday School at my own village Baptist chapel as a young child but when we turned seven—*or was it eight?*—we "didn't have to go anymore." All the kids on the street went. It's how our parents got rid of us every Sunday morning. The only other church I'd ever been to was our village Anglican church, for christenings, weddings, and "carols by candlelight" services. But only if the village schoolkids were performing a nativity play, or singing a carol. So I'd no idea what to expect that balmy, Sunday morning as we drove in Mark's car along narrow country lanes, bordered by seas of wheat shimmering in the breeze, on our way to Horham.

That particular Sunday, there was a visiting speaker and his opening prayer left me enrapt. As he thanked God for the sunshine, the crops growing in the fields, for Jesus, and for being together at that time, in that place, something inside me stirred. Deep inside. I'd never heard anyone talk to God like He really existed before. And I needed to know He did.

The rest of the service is a blur. I just recall that opening prayer, the weather, and countryside that we drove through on the way there…and that there was going to be a tent mission the following Sunday, and we were all going again.

He's tired of feeling everything about him is wrong. His weight, his gender, his loves, his personality. Everything, except, maybe, his intelligence…and his love of tennis. Whenever he can, he escapes to the tennis court (but that requires someone to play with) or just plays by himself against a wall, imagining he's at Wimbledon beating Bjorn Borg or Jimmy Connors. Or he escapes into his world of music.

Music was my first love, and it will be my last. To live without my music would be impossible to do. 'Cause in this world of trouble, my music pulls me through.[1]

But tennis and music don't fill the void within. Astrology doesn't fill it either, though it briefly gives him hope. Neither does Rosicrucianism. They don't ease the anguish he feels every day. They don't stop that image of himself in the grave. Forgotten. Perhaps something else will? Something he hasn't already tried? He's only in his early-mid teens, so there's still hope. *Isn't there?* But that image…of himself…in the grave, has been with him for so many years now. Seven? *Or is it eight?*

The next Sunday, Julie, Mark, and I headed to Horham again, to a large white tent in a field near the Baptist church. I'd never been to a tent mission before and I don't recall much

---

[1] John Miles, *Music* (1976)

of the service, except that I knew Jesus was real and I wanted Him…needed Him.

I think I always had, kinda, believed in Him. After all, there were those times when I didn't want to do cross country at school, so I prayed it would rain, and it did. And the time I was scared my art teacher was going to yell at me, so I prayed, and he didn't.

But that "god" had been distant. And those prayers felt just like the tennis balls I hit against the wall, that bounced back to me. Bjorn and Jimmy weren't really there, and perhaps God hadn't really been there too.

Now, as I felt His presence around me, I knew He was there. So I asked Him in, gently, quietly, so that no-one would even have noticed. I hardly noticed myself.

He's nearly given up hope. The image of the grave hasn't gone and he's nearly an adult now. He's tried just about everything. At least he has a new friend. But that just seems to make the alone times even more painful. *What's the point? Wouldn't I be better off dead? If I'm just going to die and be forgotten, what does it matter? No one cares if I'm dead or alive anyway.*

When I headed off to college that summer, leaving Julie, Mark, and my childhood behind, I was a Christian. But I still had no idea what God had in store for me. I'd always been a very unhappy child, though there was nothing wrong with my life that an outsider would have noticed. Nothing but a primary school headmaster who'd emotionally abused and belittled me, that is. But he'd retired when I was nine. *Or was it eight?*

I'd always asked questions about the meaning of life, but now God had given me a purpose and was slowly—very slowly—changing me. I felt less awkward, though was still shy. But so many of the questions that had plagued me when I was younger were now answered. God took away my trying to figure it all out myself and taught me to just trust Him.

He's a Christian now and happier than he's ever been, but he still feels like there's an unbreakable dam inside blocking the abundant life God promises. *Surely there's more to His life than this? Surely God, the God of the Bible, wants to transform my life completely and utterly? Surely there's more than just waiting for Heaven?*

I was at home, aware of my housemates watching TV, and I could hear the occasional car going by and strangers walking down the street. All of them oblivious to the twenty-one-year-old lying there alone, horizontal on his bed, completely unaware of what God was about to do.

As I lay there, praying, God burst in…completely, powerfully, unexpectedly. That dam came crashing down as all of the life He had promised, but that I was too scared to hope for, came flooding in. I was inundated with overwhelming emotion. For so many years, even after knowing Him, I had felt trapped. I'd felt that *life* was close but frustratingly out of reach. Now the dam had been breached, all of the baggage I had been carrying around since my childhood was washed away. My fears, my insecurities. Even an image that had held me bound since I was seven (*it wasn't even eight*) was swept away.

You see, that seven-year-old in the grave was me. That hopeless teenager was me. That desperate young adult was me.

But that boy, now a man, is still in the grave. He has died with Christ, is buried with Him through baptism and it is no longer he who lives but Christ lives in me. Through His grace, I have been saved. Amazing, amazing grace.

Ian was born and bred in the rural county of Suffolk, England but feels very much at home on the west coast. Ian contributes regularly to Inspire's blog and is currently working on his first non-fiction book.

UNMERITED FAVOR—GRACE

Julie Blackman

What did I do to deserve Jesus dying on the cross in my place?

Absolutely nothing.

Would Jesus say I was worth the cost of His precious blood?

Definitely yes.

What do I call this loving, sacrificial act?

Unmerited favor—grace.

Can I repay Him in any way?

No, never.

What can I do?

Accept Him as Lord and Savior and live for Him.

Julie Blackman writes nonfiction and fiction inspirational pieces. Her work is published in **Inspire Victory, Inspire Promise, Inspire Forgiveness, Inspire Love, Inspire Joy,** *and* **Inspire Kindness.** *Julie also writes for FaithWriters.com. Her passion for writing has grown and writing about the Lord is her desire.*

Learning from Grace

Jasmine Schmidt

Samuel tossed his briefcase on the dining room table and reached up to loosen his tie. The trial hadn't gone as he had hoped. His client wouldn't get justice this time. The judge had let the kid off with a few hours of community service. That wasn't enough of a consequence. Sam recalled the relief on the defendant's mother's face and muttered to himself. His own mother would have taken the prosecutor's side if it had been him on trial. His mother was not a believer in second chances. One strike, you're out. She had drilled that into him ever since she left his father twenty years ago. Perhaps that's what made him so good at his job.

The phone rang.

"Samuel Dalton, speaking."

"Hello Mr. Dalton, I'm calling to inform you that your payment on the house is long overdue. This is your final reminder, you have until the end of the week. We will not be extending the due date any further. I'm sorry."

Silence lagged before Sam ended the call.

Great. Just what I needed today. Sam set the phone down. Grabbing the briefcase, he took out his laptop went to the necessary site to settle his dues. *There done.* He snapped the screen shut and turned his attention to the kitchen. Food. He needed food. And a shower.

Two hours later, Sam sank into the seat by the front window with a glass of sweet tea. *Peace at last.*

Ding! Dong!

"Go away." Sam groaned.

Ding! Dong!

"*Uhg,*" Sam lowered his glass onto the side table irritably, sloshing liquid over the side. Three long strides brought him to the door and he threw the door open. "What can I do for you?" he asked, his tone sharp.

"Hi. I'm Cali. My mom lives next door so we're going to be neighbors."

"I'm sorry. Have we met before? Your voice sounds familiar," Sam interrupted. He didn't recognize anything about her, except the voice.

To his surprise Cali threw her head back and laughed, "Well that's a new one." Her eyes danced, "No, we've not met."

"I'm almost certain I've heard your voice," Sam insisted.

"Well you know my name, but I've yet to hear yours." Cali cocked her head, brushing aside his statement.

"Sam Dalton." He extended his hand.

"Oh dear." Cali grimaced as she shook his hand. "I stand corrected, Mr. Dalton. It seems I spoke to you a few hours ago on the phone." Cali paused, watching the confusion grow on Sam's face. "I called regarding your rental payment."

Sam nearly shut the door as it came back to him. It had been the same voice. Her voice was softer in person and she was a hundred times prettier than the cold hearted business woman he had imagined.

"So you're hounding me at my house now are you?" Sam narrowed his eyes. "A little unprofessional don't you think?"

"Oh goodness, I'm not here about that. I didn't know you lived here. Well I didn't know Sam Dalton lived here that is," Cali stopped herself. "I simply came to say hello, is all."

"Hello then. Now if you'll excuse me, I've got stuff to do." Sam didn't wait for a response before slamming the door.

What is wrong with you, Samuel? His conscience nagged.

Knock! Knock!

Sam glanced over at his front door. *Whoever could that be?* Sipping his coffee once more, Sam walked over and opened the front door. His shoulders sagged as he saw Cali standing on his welcome mat.

"Don't shut the door. I have a peace offering." Cali held up a plate of scones. "Freshly baked."

Peace offering? You should be bringing her scones; you were the rude one. The voice inside reminded him.

"Thanks." Sam accepted the plate and sighed inwardly. "Would you care to come inside? I have a fresh pot of coffee ready."

Cali's eyes brightened. "I never say no to a cup of coffee."

Sam stood back, allowing Cali to come inside. He followed her to the kitchen and grabbed a mug.

"Cream?" He asked, pausing from filling the mug to the top.

"No thank you."

Sam topped it off and handed the steaming cup of coffee to her. Cali held the mug in both hands, smelling the coffee and enjoying the first sip. She nodded her approval and settled on one of the counter height chairs. Sam leaned his hip against the counter and tried to come up with a conversation starter.

"So what do you do for a living Mr. Dalton?" Cali beat him to it.

"Please, call me Sam." He set down his mug. "I'm a lawyer."

"Ah, a lawyer. Interesting profession."

"It suits me." Sam shrugged. "I like seeing justice done."

Cali raised her eyebrows. Her lips parted as if she was about to speak, but then pressed back together in a firm line.

"What?" Sam straighted.

"I gather you aren't a big fan of grace then?"

"Not sure I even know what that word means anymore." Sam shrugged. "My job is to see that justice is done, not for grace to be given."

"Hmm." Cali sipped her coffee.

"Besides, grace had no place in my life and I turned out just fine." Sam turned his body to face her completely and rested an elbow on the counter. He nearly chuckled at the mixed disbelief and pity that clouded Cali's face. She didn't even seem to be trying to hide it from him. He expected her to try and convince him otherwise but Cali held her tongue and finished off her cup of coffee.

It became a frequent occurrence for Sam to share a cup of coffee with Cali. She even invited him over to her mother's for supper. Sam enjoyed her company immensely, even if Cali had strong opinions. She liked to talk about the things that really mattered in life instead of the superficial small talk. Sam found himself sharing life stories he hadn't ever told anyone. No one had ever cared to listen to them.

They sat on his small patio, sharing a fresh summer smoothie Sam had prepared. Cali was stretched in the lounge chair, face turned up to the sun, a smile on her face. She put her hand up to shade the sun from her eyes and turned to look at him. "You really believe your life has never had one ounce of grace in it?"

"What?" Sam sat up.

"When we first met I asked you about grace and you said grace had no place in your life. You truly believe that?"

"Oh." Sam slumped back against the back of the chair. "Yeah."

"What makes you think so?" Cali was sitting now.

"Just haven't seen it in my life." Sam shrugged one shoulder.

"So it wasn't grace that you didn't get benched on the basketball team when your grades dropped below requirements?"

"It was the championship, they needed me...and I wasn't the only one who didn't get benched because of grades," Sam retorted.

"That's called grace. They didn't *need* you. They really *wanted* you. They showed favor and let you play in the game even though you didn't deserve it," Cali said matter-of-factly. "I'm sure that's not the only time you've been shown grace if you really were to think on it."

"Fine. Whatever," Sam grumbled.

"You were recently shown grace." Cali wiggled an eyebrow, a smile twitching in the corner of her mouth.

Sam rolled his eyes. "How?"

"The extension on your rental payments." Cali ran her finger around the rim of her smoothie glass. "Do you know what we call those?"

"No. But I'm sure you're about to tell me," Sam murmured.

"They're called 'grace periods.'"

"Okay, okay, you've made your point." Sam sighed heavily. His mind gripped onto everything she said and fumbled through memories where grace had been shown. The little things. The big. He began to realize he had been so fixated on the times grace hadn't been shown that that's all he could remember.

"Doesn't that give you hope for the future?" Cali asked softly. "It gives me hope."

"I guess so." Sam thought hard.

"It also makes me want to show grace to others, like I've been shown grace."

Sam felt his stomach knot. He definitely hadn't shown grace to others. His mind wandered back to the trial he had lost when he first met Cali. Instead of feeling upset over his loss, Sam felt a sense of gladness that the kid had been shown grace.

"I'm sorry...I shouldn't have pushed the subject." Cali bit her lip. She threw her legs to one side of the chair and prepared to get up.

"No, thanks for bringing it up, Cali." Sam nodded. "I've lived long enough thinking cold justice was the only response to a wrong. I suppose there's justice that can be done with grace as well. It would be a pretty miserable world without grace, wouldn't it?"

"Oh yes, miserable indeed."

"Thank you, Cali."

"You are very welcome."

*Jasmine writes historical fiction novels for young adults, short stories, and poetry. She has been published in **Inspire Love** and **Inspire Kindness**. Jasmine loves reading and hanging out.*

GRACE FOR YOUR DEEPEST NEED

Christine L'Heureux

I stare in disbelief at the woman sitting calmly behind her desk. Her words abruptly shake my world. I feel as though she has just pronounced a death sentence on my dreams. She isn't being unfair or unkind, but I hoped she would make an exception.

"You need $500 more to pay your school fees for this semester. If you don't pay by Friday, you'll have to leave school."

So, is this how it's all going to end?

Will my dream of graduating from Prairie Bible Institute end today just as my senior year was beginning? I am so determined to complete four years of Bible school in Three Hills, Alberta, Canada. I have to finish! I know what's at stake. God is calling me to be a missionary. I must graduate from this missionary training school or go home as a failure.

I knew God called me to be a missionary when I was in middle school. No voice or verse from the Bible told me that. I knew in my heart. Following that vision was the hard part. I loved God and wanted to obey Him, but my heart was wounded in early childhood. My father was mentally ill, and my mother eventually divorced him. I reacted to my life circumstances with anger and bitterness. I felt I was not able to live as God wanted me to. I gave up trying and sought comfort in alcohol and drugs. My heart longed for love and acceptance. Thank God, He did not abandon me.

My Abba Father met me at an evangelistic meeting in Portland, Oregon in 1973. David Wilkerson, author of *The Cross and the Switchblade*, presented a call to repentance and new life. By God's grace, He lifted me out of my hopelessness and set me on the solid rock of His love. I was forgiven!

I told my story of rebellion and looking for love and comfort apart from God to a counselor at the meeting, and he said, "You'll never make it as a Christian unless you commit yourself one hundred percent." Now I felt that I had to live the Christian life by my determination and will. That never worked before, but I was going to try. I didn't yet understand my Abba Father's love and grace even though I had repented of my sin and trusted Christ to forgive me.

I struggled to believe I was worthy of such love. I felt different from other Christians. I thought they were all victorious over sin. I focused on sin and wanting to be free. "Try harder" was my mantra, but I couldn't fully believe in my heart that I would ever be able to please the Father.

Even though I struggled with believing God's unconditional love, my direction was clear. Go to Bible school and be a missionary. My pastor in Portland, Oregon encouraged me to go to Prairie Bible Institute (PBI) for my training.

I loved studying at PBI. I loved the caring teachers and staff, my fellow classmates, and my classes. But I was also miserable because I studied the Bible every day and saw I did not measure up to God's holy standards. I saw law not grace.

Now here I was back for my final year at PBI. I worked so hard in my studies. I had grown in my understanding of

God and forgiving others, and I learned so much from summer mission trips to Japan and to Northern Canada reaching out to Cree Indians. I learned about serving cross-culturally. I diligently worked in the school dining room to raise money for school. I did everything that I could, but I still didn't have enough money.

I went to the Finance office and told the woman there about my situation. If I couldn't pay the $500, I would have to leave school.

I was devastated. I wanted to graduate with my class and follow God wholeheartedly to cross-cultural missions. All that seemed impossible now. I cried as I walked out toward the Three Hills, actually three bumps on the horizon ahead. On my left I slowly approached the PBI-owned chicken, dairy, and pig farm. I enjoyed going there to see the animals.

On this walk, however, I did not reach the farm to find comfort among the animals.

Instead I noticed the beauty of the wildflowers growing in the ditch and in the field to my left. I began to pick them and smell them. They had different scents. I knew what my Father was trying to tell me. The fragrance of Christ would flow through my life. My unique life. I would be *to God the fragrance of Christ* (2 Corinthians 2:15 NKJV).

Just as I was bubbling over with joy and picking more flowers, a man rode up on his bicycle. He said, "I like wild flowers, too. I'm a beekeeper." I didn't tell him why I was so excited about the flowers.

We talked awhile. As he turned to ride away, he said, "Even the dandelions, I like!"

Oh, those words! Playful, with a touch of humor. Just as if the Lord Himself said them to me with a twinkle in His eye. I might feel like a weed, a dandelion, but Jesus liked me, too!

His life and fragrance would flow through me. I would fulfill my purpose!

Graduation from Bible school wasn't the important thing anymore. That encounter with the Lord amongst the wildflowers and through the beekeeper's words changed everything. At that moment it was no longer just about me. My life is about Jesus and me in intimate, loving relationship so that His glory is seen. What amazing grace!

Abba Father did provide for my financial needs through Canadian friends. I graduated and worked as a missionary for about eighteen years with OMF International in Japan. And that's another awesome grace story.

Ever wonder what God is up to in your life? When He doesn't seem to follow the plan you thought He gave you? Or when dreams shatter? Or when…? Well, how about one thousand possible scenarios that open the door for daughters and sons of the Father to question and doubt His love?

However, for you, dear friend, just one specific circumstance causes you to lose sleep. Perhaps even suffer with relentless, excruciating emotional and spiritual pain. What in the world is our loving Father doing?

What I've learned is that there are two perspectives to every difficult circumstance: my limited perspective, and God's eternal perspective.

I now imagine God's perspective on my lack of finances might have sounded something like this:

Look! Our daughter's heart is now open to Us. She'll hear Us speak. Our longing for her love and her longing for Us will connect in deeper intimacy. She'll understand that graduation is not what will satisfy her soul.

Above all, her heart is thirsty for relationship with Us. She deeply desires to be on a mission with Us. Everything will change when she experiences what her heart longs for most. Let's give her a taste of Our own joy and love.

My perspective starts out with shame, "not enough" thinking. "I am not enough. I don't have enough. I can't do enough."

Then there's God's side: *My grace is sufficient for you* (2 Corinthians 12:9 ESV).

Experiencing that grace leads to what God is *always* up to—drawing you close for relationship with Him. Here's the pattern:

- An unwelcome, confusing circumstance happens that causes great pain—often conflicting with the portrait of a gracious and loving Father.
- Because of the pain and doubting His love, we seek comfort and relief from pain but not from the Father.
- Faithfully, He draws us close, and finally we turn to Him.
- Our hearts connect and He communicates His love and grace.
- We commune with Him and express our trust and love to Him.
- The Lord reveals Himself to us in a way we can understand.
- He captures our hearts, and we move through the circumstance in Him with gratitude and joy.
- We are on a mission with Him. He works in us and through us to reveal His love and grace to others.

The grace of intimacy with the Father, Jesus, and the Holy Spirit changes everything! Circumstances may not change, but in Him we find what satisfies the aching abyss in our hearts.

He looks deeply into your heart and knows what will speak to you and capture your heart. A field of wild flowers and a beekeeper may not touch your heart. However, He knows what grace will draw your heart into deeper intimacy with Him.

My dearly loved friend, the Father says to you, "I love you as much as I love My Son" (John 17:23 paraphrase).

Prayer: "Abba Father, reveal your heart of love and grace to me so that I can experience deeper intimacy with You."

Christine L'Heureux is passionate about knowing Abba Father's heart and sharing His heart with others. She longs to experience a continuing, deeper intimacy with the Holy Trinity. God called her to serve in Japan for about eighteen years to learn and teach the love and grace of God.

OASIS

Terri Hellard-Brown

<hr/>

The oasis of a kind and loving heart
Offering water to a parched and guilty soul
Refreshing friendship
Broken by careless words
The healing of deep wounds
Cracked open in the desolation of lost love
Cool water poured over an agonizing heart
Left homeless and alone in the vast, empty landscape of life
Abundant life like a palm flourishing beside the water
Even though surrounded by hot, gritty sand
Hope in a dry, thirsty land
That seldom shows anyone mercy
In a world full of prickly jabs and hateful barbs
The soft place that envelopes us
Surrounding, holding, welcoming us home
This is grace

Terri Hellard-Brown

Terrie, a California native, grew up in Oklahoma, was a missionary in Taiwan, and has settled in Sacramento. She's a writer, teacher, wife, and mom. But mostly, she's a Christian trying to live her faith. She's been published several times. Favorite topic is Christian life, and she's written children's stories.

GET OUT NOW!

Karen Polk

"I don't want you! I don't need you! Just get out of my life!" the young man shouted with anger toward God. He flicked on the computer and threw himself into the chair. Staring hard at the screen, he waited impatiently for the characters of the game to show themselves. His phone buzzed with messages. Probably family trying to get ahold of him. He didn't care. Why should he?

After two hours of online playing, Jay had won the game again. But somehow, this time, it didn't matter. Leaning back in the chair, he pulled his dog onto his lap and held her tight. Lately, it had become his ritual. Check out of reality; mentally turn into a game character, and zone out for hours at a time. It kept him from thinking. It eased the pain. It covered the hurt. And yet somehow he felt so empty. So lonely. So alone.

Jay began taking his time getting home from his job each day. It meant less time on the computer. More time to shout at God.

"Why does it hurt so bad, God?" he shouted in the cab of his truck as he banged on the steering wheel. "Why won't You help me? I hate my life! I hate what I've become!"

Family chaos, wrong choices, huge financial debt, a "couldn't care less" attitude, and anger! How could he not hate life? And yet...

With an hour's drive home, he turned the music on low and allowed his thoughts to drift. It had been months since the day he talked to his parents and shared with them his wrong lifestyle choices. He could still see their faces as if it were yesterday. He had burdened them with news they didn't want or need to hear. He had placed a lot of the blame of his life issues on them. But Mom just slowly and quietly hung her head with great sadness on her face. Dad spoke softly, gently, telling him they would continue to love him no matter what. *How could they respond so quietly?* he thought. Guilt made him stay away. He had not gone back to visit since that heartbreaking evening.

Jay sat parked in the driveway after arriving at his small mobile home. It was a reminder of how he lived, escaping from reality and sinking deeper into despair. He wanted out and knew who would help, but shame kept him from making the call.

At last, he trudged in. He opened his arms wide for his excited four-legged greeter to jump into and held her tight, in his arms once again, feeling like she was the only stable part of his life that he could count on. Foregoing the computer game, he kicked off his boots and climbed in bed, not caring that it was only eight o'clock. He wanted to close his eyes and forget it all.

The loud shrill startled Jay awake! Sitting up quickly, he tried to locate where the noise was coming from. Realizing it was his cell phone alarm he reached for it, knocking a glass of water to the floor. Shattered! Just like his life.

Tiptoeing in bare feet, he fumbled to find a light. It had been a fitful night of sleep and he felt just as exhausted as when he fell into bed the night before. *What day was it anyway? Saturday. No wait! Sunday. Easter Sunday!* His boss had told him as he left work the day before that he would need to go check on an oilrig out in the field. Yes, even on Easter. Being a mechanic for the oilrigs meant being on call most days. It was no big deal, really. It would mean double pay. It would mean being out of the house. It would mean a way to forget about family and emotional pain. Yes, just another workday.

Until recently, Jay thought life was great living on his own, doing as he pleased, without anyone nearby to point out the wrongs. He had imagined his parents with sleepless nights and appetites gone, fearful for him. But he hadn't cared. Anger and bitterness consumed him. But what he didn't know was that his parents had set up a prayer campaign on his behalf involving family and friends. With their cell phone alarms set, they were going to "fight" for him through prayer, daily, at 12:30.

As Jay drove to the oilrig that Easter Sunday, in which it seemed he was the only lone one on the road, he couldn't deny the truth in his heart any longer. He was ashamed of all he had done and how he had turned his back on God when life seemed to spin out of control. And he was mad at himself for the damage he had caused in his family relationships.

The loving words from both his parents floated about continually in his mind causing the turmoil and struggle in his heart to become increasingly tormenting. He could sense God wasn't giving up on him and neither were his parents. His happiness had plummeted, and his health suffered. Cold sores. Chest pain. Loss of appetite. And, his own sleepless nights.

A wave of conviction and regret washed over him as thoughts of his childhood teachings about God's unconditional love and forgiveness came to the forefront of his mind. He cringed in his heart as he realized that, on this very day, his parents and siblings were together celebrating the true meaning of Easter, Christ's resurrection from death on the cross. Suddenly he missed his loving family.

With the truck set to cruise control, he began to cry out to God, begging His forgiveness and imploring how he might make things right.

During the next few days, a strong battle raged in his heart and mind. He was torn between listening to the negative thoughts of despair and God firmly nudging him to turn back to Him.

He could stand it no longer. He had enough of this mind and heart battle. He was giving in. Done!

He pushed the send button, waiting and wondering.

"How will he respond to my call?" Jay whispered quietly to no one. "Will he help me?" By now his heart was pounding. "Stupid question! Of course, he will. He's my dad. And a caring one," he mumbled, answering his own question.

Hearing the familiar voice answer on the other end, Jay stammered sheepishly, "Dad? Uh...I...want to come home."

"And we want you home," came the calm reply. "Gather your personal belongings and get out of your home now before you change your mind. We'll be anxiously awaiting your arrival."

"I'll do whatever you tell me to do, Dad." And with that, Jay hung up. Walking away from his wrong lifestyle wasn't going to be easy, but his heart was already feeling lighter and he couldn't wait for the workday to be over.

The drive to his parents' home seemed longer than usual and he couldn't help but think over and over about how his mom would receive him. Her look of sadness at his news those months ago hung so clear before his eyes.

But he needn't have worried. At the sound of his truck, she came out running, pulling him into her open arms.

And, the sign on the window? "Welcome Home, Son!"

Yes, it felt good to be home!

Karen Polk is a writer who turns real life experiences into stories that will encourage the readers. She also enjoys writing devotionals and teaching Women's Bible Studies. Karen and her husband enjoy the outdoors together and time with their six children. She is currently employed with Visiting Angels.

THERE, BUT FOR THE GRACE OF GOD...

Christine Hagion

"My wife is going to prison," my husband said with a smirk. "I told everyone at work, and they all asked me, 'how long is she in for?' and 'what did your wife do, that she had to go to prison'?"

I chuckled at his joke while setting out the thermos that would help me survive the three-hour drive to the institution in the wee hours in the morning. I laid out my clothes for the next day, making sure the pants I had chosen had no rivets and the bra had no underwire to cause an alarm at the security desk's metal scanners.

I double-checked the bag I'd packed: handouts, pens, nametags for the workshop I'd be teaching, along with a small black zippered pouch with all the essentials for three days (toothpaste, toothbrush, medications, lip balm, and aspirin), just in case I was detained due to a lock-down. I felt excited and a little nervous to be going to the women's prison, where I would be training thirty hand-picked inmates to become peer educators and advocates to raise awareness about abuse—the first program of its kind in the country.

I shook my head at the irony of it all. A woman from church had asked me what I had in common with the inmates, and at first, I didn't have an answer. But following her question, I remembered instances I had long ago put out of my memory...

One Christmas morning, when I was eleven, I bounded into my mother's bedroom, stocking in hand, and jumped up and down on the mattress. But I was shocked to find my sister, Helen*, under the covers instead of my mother. Hank*, my mom's live-in boyfriend, popped his head out from under the sheet. My stocking dropped onto the floor, and the orange that had been tucked inside it rolled under the bed. The joy of the holiday instantly drained out of me, and I forgot all about goodwill toward men.

"It's okay, Sissy. Really, it is." Helen tried to reassure me, ignoring the reality of the ugly situation. Lost in a dream world, she said, "Hank loves me. We're going to get married." I stared at her young, innocent face as she gazed adoringly at Hank's greasy head on the pillow. I wanted to scream.

A short man in his late thirties, Hank couldn't read much, as he'd only made it to the sixth grade. He never seemed able to hold down a job for more than a few weeks. Most of his teeth had been knocked out in frequent drunken brawls over the years. Hank spoke with a country twang, and when he talked, only three yellowed front teeth were visible. He reminded me of Festus on the old TV western, *Gunsmoke*. Hank used about a pound of styling gel in his hair, chain-smoked, and guzzled vodka as if it were Kool-Aid®. *What can Helen possibly see in him?*

"Hank is going to marry Mom," I countered. "And anyway, Helen, you're only fifteen years old! He couldn't marry you right now, even if he wanted to."

The hopeful look in her face darkened with my words.

"He's lying to you, Sis," I continued. "He's old enough to be your father. This isn't love, and marrying him wouldn't make it right, even if he *could* do it." I glared at him. I was so angry at Hank that I could not contain myself. I ran out of the room to keep from exploding in front of her.

Many questions ran through my mind: *How long has this been going on? Does Mom know? Why does Helen give herself away to this hillbilly? How can she throw her life away like this? And how can this go on, right under my mother's nose?*

I learned that Hank had been molesting my sister for some time. He had taken Helen out into the backyard tool shed, where they "did it" in the midst of pitchforks, hedge trimmers, shovels, rakes, and rotting wood. The thought of it made me sick to my stomach. *How can she possibly think this is love?*

I wanted to kill him. If I have ever known what demons drive someone to murder, I was introduced to them then. I went into that tool shed myself, their "love shack," and vomited. Then I seized an axe.

I stole one of Hank's favorite cowboy shirts and wrapped it around a tree. I vented my rage at Hank on the innocent tree, imagining his face as I swung the axe with all my might, again and again. Its mangled trunk, and his shirt, now reduced to ribbons blowing in the wind, served as a warning to him to watch his back.

Four years later, Hank stood over my mother as she lay unconscious on the floor in the hallway. Neither of us were sure whether she had passed out in a drunken stupor, or whether this beating had knocked her out. Hank repeatedly kicked her motionless body with his steel-toed boots, and I knew I had to protect her.

"You're going to kill her if you don't stop," I yelled. He drew his leg back, showing that he had no intention of ending his attack. I ran into the kitchen, grabbed a chopping knife, and pointed it toward his belly. "If you don't leave her alone right now, I'll gut you like a fish." Hank's eyes darted from me, to the knife, and back at her. He hesitated for an excruciatingly tense moment, then turned and walked away.

Following this incident, I was made a ward of the state, and was housed temporarily in a group home with other troubled teenagers. Months after the court's decision that I should be placed in foster care permanently, I was allowed a half-hour visit in our old home, with my social worker present. As my mother sat in her recliner, I noted the telltale marks of abuse. The bluish imprint of Hank's cowboy boot on her upper arm told me nothing had changed while I was gone. During this visit, I discovered that the fire which almost destroyed the house was not caused by faulty electrical wiring, but because Hank had tried to set the mattress on fire while she was passed out on the bed. Foster care was a definite improvement from my childhood home.

A lifetime later, I am filled with gratitude that by God's grace, I escaped that hellish existence. When I was unable to help myself, God rescued me from that chaos.

So now, when I minister in the prison, I have compassion toward the inmates, knowing that like me, some of them resorted to violence in a desperate attempt to save someone they loved from further harm. With the clarity that comes with hindsight, I realize now that Hank could easily have taken the knife away from me and stabbed me, or I could have killed him and spent the rest of my life in prison. I have learned that violence is not the solution to abuse, and now I am able to show the prisoners that there are more peaceful alternatives. There, but for the grace of God, go I.

*not their real names

Christine Hagion is an ordained minister, counselor, author, and advocate. For over twenty years she has worked with people experiencing family violence, and her work reflects the wisdom she's gained from her clients. Known as "Dr. Red," she seeks to raise awareness about these issues in writing and speaking. www. RevRedPhD.com.

INDEX OF CONTRIBUTORS

Index of Contributors

Inspire Press is a division of
INSPIRE CHRISTIAN WRITERS

Inspire Christian Writers provides a network of support, encouragement, education, and spiritual growth for Christian writers. We minister biblical truths with excellence, clarity, and love, to transform lives and the publishing industry. To learn more and/or join, please visit **inspirewriters.com**

Also available from Inspire Press
INSPIRE TRUST, 2012
INSPIRE FAITH, 2013
FRIENDS OF INSPIRE FAITH, 2013
INSPIRED GLIMPSES OF GOD'S PRESENCE, 2013
INSPIRE VICTORY, 2014
INSPIRE PROMISE, 2014
INSPIRE FORGIVENESS, 2015
INSPIRE JOY, 2016
INSPIRE LOVE, 2017
INSPIRE KINDNESS, 2018
Exit Cyrus, 2014
DogSpirations, 2015
How to Love God with All Your Heart, 2015
The Never Ending Gifts, 2016
Days of Faith and Joy, 2018
How to Build an In-Law House in California, 2019

Coming Fall 2020 ~ INSPIRE ADVENTURE

To receive submission guidelines and/or
publication information, please email
inspirepress@inspirewriters.com

CPSIA information can be obtained
at www.ICGtesting.com
Printed in the USA
FSHW020906191119

9 781938 196164